Also by Ed Barks

A+ Strategies for C-Suite Communications:
Turning Today's Leaders into Tomorrow's Influencers

The Truth About Public Speaking:
The Three Keys to Great Presentations

REPORTERS
DON'T YOU
HATE

ED BARKS

Reporters Don't Hate You:
100+ Amazing Media Relations Strategies
By Ed Barks

Published by:
Ogmios Publishing
Berryville, Virginia

eBook ISBN 978-0-9742538-0-0
Paperback ISBN 978-0-9742538-1-7
Library of Congress Control Number: 2020910964

This publication is designed to provide accurate and authoritative information in regard to the subject matter covered. It is sold with the understanding that the publisher is not engaged in rendering legal, accounting, or other professional service. If legal advice or other expert assistance is required, the services of a competent professional person should be sought.
– From a Declaration of Principles jointly adopted by a committee of the American Bar Association and a Committee of Publishers and Associations

Discounts for bulk purchases are available for corporate and association meetings, professional societies, and book clubs. Call (540) 955-0600 to make arrangements.

Ed Barks is available to speak at your next annual meeting, conference, or retreat, in person or via video link. To learn more, visit www.barkscomm.com/speaker or call (540) 955-0600.

Keep up to date with the latest from Ed by signing up for his Communications Community newsletter at www.barkscomm.com/comms-community.

Ed likes to hear from his readers. Email him at ebarks@barkscomm.com. Visit him online at www.barkscomm.com.

Print edition includes index

Advance Praise for *Reporters Don't Hate You*

"As a former reporter who transitioned to public relations, Ed Barks offers practical and straightforward advice to anyone who is fearful of the media. His basic premise of 'walk in a reporter's shoes' is such a simple thought, but is often lost when reporters try to get basic information from corporate executives, athletes, celebrities, civic leaders, or politicians. Ed doesn't mince words and offers a treasure trove of good ideas. It's a must-have for anyone trying to figure out how the media work – and how they can become a pro at mastering media relations."
— Cornelius "Neil" Foote, Jr., president, National Black Public Relations Society

"*Reporters Don't Hate You* feels like an AP Style guide for media relations. Mine will be dog-eared!"
— Deanne Yamamoto, agency veteran

"How do business executives protect themselves and their businesses from bad reporting? Simple: by being a good source and molding the message early. Ed Barks explains how that's done, point by point. This is media training on steroids, written in a very easy-to-read and precise format."
— Rick Pullen, former editor in chief of *Leader's Edge* magazine

"Drawing on years of field-tested experience, Ed Barks has given communications and media relations professionals a trove of practical and compelling advice on how to manage interviews and elevate your key messages to the top of any story. *Reporters Don't Hate You: 100+ Amazing Media Relations Strategies* is a must-have desktop reference for anyone who deals with the press."
— Dr. Glenn Cummings, President, The University of Southern Maine

"Ed Barks has put together a book that should be on the reading list not just of media professionals, but also for journalists."
— Gil Klein, director University of Oklahoma's Washington Journalism Program and past president of the National Press Club

"Every page is chock-full of helpful advice and insights that anyone who works with the media should read and remember. Now there is only one reason why you should ever be surprised or disappointed when you are interviewed by a reporter – because you did not read *Reporters Don't Hate You* before the interview."
— Edward Segal, crisis management expert, consultant, and author of *Crisis Ahead: 101 Ways to Prepare for and Bounce Back from Disasters, Scandals, and Other Emergencies*

"Ed Barks provides communications insights, advice and feedback that are meaningful and useful to executives facing the news media. He really has helped our organization 'sharpen the saw' when it comes to delivering on-target messages that amplify our key priorities."
— Melissa Hockstad, President and CEO, *American Cleaning Institute*

As always, to Celeste and Polly, who make life worth living.

And to my radio role models who taught me what the media is all about –
Jim Cameron, Mike Shalett, and Roger Stauss.

CONTENTS

PREFACE

This is not the book I had intended to publish next. That was the least of my — or certainly the world's — concerns when the coronavirus pandemic struck.

I had already begun initial research into my planned third book focusing on critical communications and public affairs issues. March and April were to be the months for interviews with experts and research at the Library of Congress. It became clear in March 2020 that this illness was evolving into something far more serious than any of us had ever dealt with (baseball fan that I am, the gravity of the situation really hit home when Major League Baseball closed down spring training). Suddenly, no one had either the time or the inclination to talk. Then the Library of Congress closed its reading rooms.

Naïvely as it turns out, I forecast that, within a week or two, people would be accustomed to working from home. They would be bored and ready to engage for a 20- to 30-minute interview that would get their name in a book as an expert source. That didn't happen (and taught me the current futility of trying to shape any business plans for even the near term).

So I turned to a shorter book, one I could publish quickly in hopes it would provide aid during the crisis and beyond.

I thankfully count myself among the fortunate. My wife and I have been in isolation for three months and counting as I write this. We still enjoy one another's company. Our daughter and her husband are safe and healthy, albeit distant from us.

We have been able to make contributions to a number of charitable groups, in particular those that feed children in need and address social justice issues. While I cannot help but think that these donations are a mere drop in the bucket in the big picture, we are all doing what we can when we can in these times.

Reporters Don't Hate You represents a small contribution of another sort, one I hope will prove helpful to communications experts, fellow professionals who have given much to me over the years.

You have my sincerest wish that this volume serves as your reliable guide to strengthen your media relations capabilities.

INTRODUCTION

There is this theory that reporters and their news sources are adversaries, sometimes even viewed as mortal enemies. I admit to falling into this trap at times.

It is, of course, utter nonsense. Remove the company spokesperson from the face of the earth and reporters would have no foundation for their stories. Subtract the journalists and companies would be hard pressed to get their message out to the public courtesy of a vetted, and more or less objective, third party.

This point was recently driven home to me by Alan Bjerga. I've known Alan for more than a decade. He is an experienced journalist and a former president of the National Press Club who recently crossed over into the communications realm. I interviewed him for one of my C-suite Blueprint Radio programs, and asked what led him to hop the fence. He explained that he didn't view the separation between the press and a company's advocates as a fence or barrier. It was a matter of using similar skills in another context. What a refreshing take.

I spent nine years serving on the board of governors of the National Press Club. From day one, my primary goal was to build bridges between the two membership constituencies there – journalists and communicators. Although the need for such bridge building will never cease, I like to think that those efforts over nearly a decade will endure and continue to prove fruitful to both professions.

Reporters Don't Hate You represents a building block in that bridge. It reinforces material for the experienced interviewee, serves as a resource for media relations experts who need additional leverage with the C-suite, performs a mentor-like function for new practitioners, and steers those reporters considering a transition to the communicator field.

There is much here for journalists, too, although I fully acknowledge that they will not agree with everything. The good ones, however, will view this as an honorable attempt to set mutually agreeable rules of the road.

This volume is intended to be an evergreen reference guide, not a current events primer. Yet it is clear that our world is evolving rapidly and unpredictably, and that can impact your media relations strategy.

The first part of 2020 witnessed stunning change. The coronavirus pandemic and resulting economic nosedive enveloped us all. Social justice also came to the fore as Black Lives Matter marches took place nationwide and gripped the world's consciousness as never before. These issues changed both our sense of the world around us and how we conduct business.

The expectation for companies to weigh in on major social issues with real commitment has never been greater. What does this mean for your media relations efforts? If you think you're going to do an interview revolving around your new product or service, you must be prepared to answer questions about social justice, race relations, gender equity, the future of our economy, and your post-pandemic designs.

Everything is fair game. Differentiating your company based on its approach to societal issues is not just the right thing to do, it is also good for business. Putting a Black Lives Matter banner on your website and calling it a day does not suffice. You've got to be ready with responses in the press that go beyond that cosmetic step.

A team of beta readers – each one an outstanding communications professional I have known for years and respect immensely – has added valuable perspectives that make this a better resource. My deepest thanks to Lloyd Brown, Ayana Burch, Dionne C. Clemons, Brian Henry, Allison Scherer, and Deanne Yamamoto. Your insights and expertise have contributed more than you know.

My thanks once again to copy editor extraordinaire Sheryl Bauerschmidt. It has been a delight working with you on these last two books and rekindling our professional relationship. Of course, any errors that remain rest strictly at the author's doorstep.

To my group of fellow independent authors that meets monthly at the National Press Club: Thank you for your support and inspiration. Together, I believe we are lighting a path that can free authors from the constraints of an often dysfunctional publishing industry.

You, dear reader, will find material intended to bolster awareness. Included is a reporter's glossary – a listing of journalistic terms of art that every communicator needs to know. Maybe you are unfamiliar with terms like bumper, lede, IFB, or VNR. You will find all that and more in Chapter Six. Thanks to journalism veterans Myron Belkind and Julie Moos for their expertise with that section.

Also incorporated are some thoughts on what you can do as we emerge from the pandemic. I fully realize that, given the rapid, day-to-day changes taking place, some of this will be rendered inoperative over time. We must all manage under the reality that we cannot now see around the corner into the future. Not that we ever could. Yet it is even more challenging today.

A handful of pointers to bear in mind as you read. I encourage you to:

- Keep this book close. Don't let it gather dust on a shelf. Use it as a reference to guide you through times routine and challenging.

- Get a copy in the hands of your colleagues – both internal and external – who stand to benefit from it. Then, foster a discussion with them. Who knows? It might even lead to the formation of a business book club.

- Jump around. There's no rule that says you have it read it from front to back. Search for what you need first, internalize that lesson, then move on to your next priority.

- Take notes. Take lots of notes. Only you know how to classify things so that they make the most sense to you.

- Get in touch with me. Some authors cringe at the thought. Not me. I love to hear from my readers. Do you have an idea for an added tip? Maybe you think something here is off base? I invite you to share your thoughts. You will find my contact information at the back of the book.

Don't give up hope. The fact is when we keep our wits about us and stay in touch with one another, we profit. Similarly, when you use the advice contained in this volume, your media relations endeavors will thrive.

Ed Barks
June 2020

CHAPTER 1

The Business Deal

Regard every interview with a reporter as a business deal. It is akin to buying anything from a loaf of bread to a new car. In those cases, the business deal involves an exchange of money. With a reporter, the business deal consists of an exchange of information. Knowledge and opinion are traded as commodities. You are the seller; the reporter is the buyer.

Thinking of each interview as a business deal helps you keep things on a professional plane, where they belong. Under no circumstance is it a good idea to take matters personally or let your anger show. Trust me, you will not win a fight with people who buy ink by the barrel or servers by the truckload, and who seek clicks by the tens or hundreds of thousands.

Emblazon this word on your brain when you agree to a media interview: Opportunity.

I emphasize an attitude of opportunity time and again when leading media training workshops. Every interview is an opportunity to spread your message to a group of people you want to reach. You should not fixate on whether the reporter likes you or not. Frankly, that doesn't matter. Remember, this is a business deal. It is your job to use the reporter as a vehicle to reach your intended audience. Each question gives you the chance to counter with a message-oriented response.

Everyone has their own unique style. Some people come across as friendly, others as authoritative, for example. Different styles work for different people.

I do not suggest that you change the way you operate. Playing to your strengths has already made you a success in your chosen field. Still, you can improve if you build upon the communications skills that got you where you are today.

Make Sustained Professional Development a Habit

Pay attention to the need for assessing feedback about your performance at every opportunity. This holds value for future business deals with reporters.

Think of learning as a process, not an event. I see all too often executives who studiously ignore the need for sustained professional development. The fact is polished communicators are dedicated lifelong learners. They realize the only way to keep their careers in forward motion involves enhancing their knowledge over time. This attitude places you, assuming you buy into the principle, as a respected media source soaring a notch above the competition.

For instance, today's savvy communicators know how to connect with reporters through their digital media channels, just as their predecessors learned how to communicate with journalists via email in the 1990s and faxes in the 1980s.

These successful individuals also realize that the development of a constructive professional development plan is imperative. You may be able to create this plan internally or you may choose to work with a media strategy and training consultant. Whatever route you take, commit to mapping out and executing your roadmap. You will find such a plan, with its emphasis on assessing feedback, becomes your guiding star if you have hopes of expanding your quotability from the trade press to *The New York Times*.

Part of a solid plan consists of periodic media training workshops that give you the brush up you need. You may require a refresher course once a year, once a month, or anything in between. The frequency depends on the range, complexity, and evolution of your issues. It is akin to your yearly physical exam; you get it whether you think you need it or not, just to be sure you are still the picture of health. A media checkup ensures your communications wellbeing.

Build some variety into your plan. For example, mix in some Q&A rehearsal with reading worthwhile resources. Add a dash of message review along with an assessment of what the media is covering today. You will find several options detailed in Chapters Four and Seven.

Due Diligence Counts

The best way to increase your odds of gaining column inches when you deal with reporters is to prepare as you would for any other business deal. For instance, a sales person wouldn't think of initiating a sales call without knowing something about their prospective customer. So it is with the press.

Your first decision is basic, yet often overlooked: Is this an interview opportunity you should accept? In most cases, you are likely to answer yes. There will be those occasions, however, when a request is off-base. Perhaps the media outlet does not reach your target audience. Or you may recognize the reporter as hostile or unethical.

Preparation also involves analyzing your ultimate audience. Remember, the reporter is merely a vehicle through which you reach your intended target. Be sure the media outlets you select are read and viewed by the people who need to hear your message.

Ascertain some basic information: How many readers or viewers does the media outlet reach? Is it a general circulation newspaper, TV morning show, trade publication, or credible blog? What is its audience's level of sophistication with respect to your issue?

If your aim is a mass audience, the major dailies and TV networks make sense. If, on the other hand, you need to reach a specific slice of your customer base, a trade publication or hyperlocal blog may be your best bet. Similarly, if you are a medical professional talking to your peers, a scientific journal is appropriate.

In essence, make sure your message is relevant to the target audience. Aim to find that intersection between what you want to say, what the current conversation is, and what viewers, listeners, and readers want to know.

Next, learn a few things about the reporter. Review articles they have written and talk to colleagues who have been interviewed by them previously. Check for a presence on such digital media tools.

Then write down the questions you anticipate and gauge which part of your message best addresses each one. This intelligence gathering phase helps you place your quotable quotes in the article.

Practice! Practice! Practice!

Clearly, the interview itself is where performance counts. But don't ignore the learning moments that take place before and after. One key to success when it comes to your advance preparation is summed up in three little words: *Practice! Practice! Practice!*

You likely hold run throughs religiously when preparing for a business pitch. Why not do the same when engaged in business deals with the media?

It is important to realize that none of us are born with the innate ability to deal with the media. It is a complex set of skills acquired over time, much like the best carpenters, IT developers, and doctors gain expertise.

An honest self-critique is fundamental. Record yourself with a video camera or your mobile phone, speak into an audio recorder, or arrange for colleagues to lob questions at you. Such practice sessions are essential.

You may view yourself on video or listen to an audio recording of your voice and think you are witnessing a stranger. This is a common occurrence. Keep in mind as you practice, what matters is how others see and hear you as you strive to impart your message.

How to Alienate a Reporter

There are certain expressions guaranteed to grate on any credible reporter. Speak any of these code words during your media business deals and you will bear responsibility for turning the interview into a negative experience.

- *"No comment."* These two small yet inflammatory words will convince reporters that you have something to hide.
- *"Why are you asking that?"* It doesn't matter why they delve into a given issue. If the question is hostile or off-point, it is up to you to redirect the interview.
- *"The earliest I can get back to you is next week."* Rapid response to media inquiries separates the pros from the wannabes. Unless the reporter has indicated the deadline is, in fact, next week, reply quickly.
- *Take the long route to answer a short question.* Like the rest of us, reporters are crunched for time. Make your answers succinct; avoid a wandering tour of your issue.
- *"Our end-to-end solutions create functionality for enterprises using IT platforms across all vertical channels."* You might as well be speaking Martian. Use plain language and leave the jargon back at the office.
- *"I'm not sure, but I would guess ... "* You are now in the process of digging a hole straight to the center of the Earth. Don't speculate. If you don't know, say so, then move on to familiar territory.
- *"I can't tell you that."* You may not be able to discuss certain issues due to legal, personnel, or proprietary concerns. Reporters understand this, but you need to tell them why you cannot discuss a specific issue while remaining open to talking about other areas.
- *"You're not going to misquote me, are you?"* This is akin to asking your doctor if they prescribed the wrong medication. Questioning a journalist's professionalism is a sure way to get on their bad side.

- *"I don't have any background material on that."* Reporters are always seeking to flesh out their stories. They may not write about all the in-depth information you give them, but your materials can help put matters into context for them.
- *"It's the media's fault."* A desperate ploy and a refuge for scoundrels who often have something to hide.
- *"That's a dumb question."* There are few dumb questions. But plenty of media sources come up with dumb answers.
- *"Tell me the name of your publication again."* If you don't know this one, you haven't done your homework and don't deserve to qualify as an expert news source.
- *"Call me back later; I'm too busy to talk to you now."* Don't sit by your phone waiting for that return call.
- *"You're just playing gotcha journalism."* If you can't stand the heat of Q&A, step out of the kitchen and let someone else do the job.
- *"I'm not the right person."* If you leave it at that, you have left the reporter hanging and missed an opportunity to get your company's story out. Always be sure to give them the name and contact information of the proper individual.
- *"But we bought advertising in your publication."* The polite term for this is "conflict of interest." Another apt expression is "stupid." Buy an ad if you want. But don't expect coverage or preferential treatment as a result.
- *"I didn't realize you wanted an on-camera interview."* When a TV producer sets up an interview, always assume it will be on camera. Dress accordingly.
- *"I'd like to review a copy of your article before it is published."* You are not the editor. Standards of good journalism dictate that news outlets have the final say (this is true in the United States; attitudes can differ in other countries). That is as it should be in a society with a free press.

Take Charge of Your Interview

You should be the one who takes charge of the direction of your business deal. Many reporters will come up with good, incisive questions. But others will cause you to wander all over the lot – if you let them. Don't.

Frame in advance the message points you need to convey to the reporter for you to consider the interview a success. What does success mean? A media report that moves you closer to attainting your business and public policy goals.

If the reporter doesn't ask you about one of your key points, it is your job to tell them. In fact, it is advisable to kick off the interview with an "opening statement" whenever possible. This should not be anything that sounds formal, canned, or rehearsed (although you will indeed want to rehearse it). Rather, it is a quick primer that helps you set the tone and orient the reporter to your terra firma.

Remember two basics. First, what does your target audience want to know? Second, what do they need to know? Answer those two questions clearly and succinctly, and your information is likely to be used by the reporter.

There are a number of ways you can assert control, in a very diplomatic manner, of course. First, adjust your way of thinking. Remind yourself that you are the expert. Take confidence in that knowledge. Reporters seek you out for a reason – you are a valued source of information they may not be able to obtain anywhere else.

Here is one more simple method to help you take charge: Speak in everyday language. Every profession has its buzzwords. Within your office walls, that is perfectly fine. But lose that jargon when you face the press.

Speak as you would to a 12-year-old. Your goal is to make your story accessible and easily understandable for the reporter's readers, viewers, or listeners. So be sure to dial your jargon meter way down.

CHAPTER 2

Develop Your Magnetic Message

In the end, the strength of your message will determine the level of success regarding your business deals with the press. A magnetic message carries the day. A weak message sags under questioning.

Your message should be built upon four strong and organized points, not a random collection of facts. Quick story: I always ask for a company's messaging in advance of a media strategy or messaging review and development workshop. Some already have elegant messages in hand; most don't. The riskiest case arises with those firms that send four to five pages of disorganized, rambling bullet points. They think they have things under control when, in reality, they are sending spokespeople out into the world confused and woefully ill-equipped.

Think of your message as a series of four main themes that can withstand the toughest questions from the biggest skeptics. As a matter of fact, one of the best ways to test the efficacy of your message is to invite the office skeptic to hurl questions at you. If your message proves responsive, congratulations. If not, head back to the drawing board.

Communications staff need to be driving this train. Experts in that discipline should be skilled at message development. If not, hire someone who knows the territory or work with a consultant who is proficient in this area.

A Chair with Four Strong Legs

I use the analogy of a chair that needs four sturdy legs to support your weight. You will hear person after person tell you that you need three points. For the simplest of messages, maybe. Still, I've done the research they probably haven't.

Why four points? That's what the findings show. While there are differences among individuals and in the complexity of a given message, literature from Nelson Cowan, Curators Distinguished Professor in the Department of Psychological Sciences at the University of Missouri, indicate that four is typically the magic number (for a complete treatment, see "The magical number 4 in short-term memory: A reconsideration of mental storage capacity" in *Behavioral and Brain Sciences*, February 2001, pp. 87-114).

If one of the four legs of your "message chair" is weak, the underpinnings fall and your story collapses. With it tumble your efforts to communicate effectively with your public. Unfortunately, too many companies ignore the health of their message until the damage is done. Don't let this happen to you. To avoid that pitfall, a messaging discussion needs to be a central part of your planning process.

The benefits of this approach go beyond media interviews. They extend to cogent messages that thread through your speeches, website content, and digital media efforts.

Consider this point as you craft your messaging. You can reasonably anticipate perhaps 90 percent of what a reporter is going to ask. It is your responsibility to put in the work to have answers for that 90 percent. The other 10 percent is the unanticipated. When questions of that nature arise, it is up to you to bridge back to one of the four legs of your message (more on this in Chapter Five).

To start building a magnetic message, you need to ask yourself some frank questions: What is the problem? Why are you the most credible person to tell your story? What is your solution? What is the next step? How does your issue affect readers or viewers? Why should they care?

What do you want them to do about it? How can you put matters into context for your audience?

Once you have settled on your four legs, build support for each with relevant facts, figures, stories, and other support mechanisms.

I have written in some detail about messaging in two previous books, so will avoid repetition here. Suffice to say there are different categories of messages and different structures appropriate to each.

In addition, you need to muster the self-discipline to stick to your narrative, and repeat and reinforce that message at every opportunity, no matter what questions the reporter asks.

Think of your message as your safe harbor. When the going gets rough and the questions become challenging or you simply lose your train of thought, set sail for safe harbor by tacking toward your message.

No question, this involves hard work and takes a fair amount of practice. But if you are committed to rising to the "A list" of media sources, you need to devote the time and energy required to develop a magnetic message.

Quotable Quotes

Once you have built your "message chair" with four solid legs, the next step is to make your story attractive enough for journalists to report it. I call these irresistible words "quotable quotes." Media relations pros know that these gems are pre-planned and well-rehearsed.

Media interviews demand memorable quotes. By adding some spice to your language, you can make your message stand out above the competition and strengthen your business deals with reporters. There are certain techniques used by people who deal with the media frequently, whether they are talking to *The Wall Street Journal*, the Today show, a small trade newsletter, their local newspaper, or a podcast host.

Following are some tools the experts use to prove the validity of their message:

- Stories – Tell a mesmerizing tale that makes your message spring to life.
- Numbers – Help your listeners size up your message with mental pictures of millions, dozens, fractions, and percentages.
- Vivid Words – Color your language with action words and phrases your audience will store in their mind's scrapbook.
- Analogies – Bring clear pictures to the mind's eye with these figures of speech.
- Extremes – Tell your listeners that you are the first, the best, the hottest, or the only (and of experiences you've had with the last or the worst).
- Case Histories – Mention true-to-life situations that have affected you and those you know.
- Third-party Endorsements – Offer testimonials from delighted clients and colleagues.
- Clichés – Use these judiciously and they can be effective.
- Topics du Jour – Sprinkle your conversation with references to current events and the latest in popular film, television, music, and sports.
- Famous Quotes – Employ words of wisdom from people you admire in the world of politics, business, the arts, and other fields.
- Jiu-Jitsu – Borrow from this ancient martial art and quote your rivals when they speak favorably of you.
- Surveys – Demonstrate why public opinion is on your side.
- Calls to Action – Urge readers and viewers to check out your new offering, visit your website, or write their Member of Congress.
- Humor – Don't tell a joke if you are a lousy joke teller. Situational humor may work better for you.

These time-tested strategies will help you land your quotable quotes in the press, successfully transmitting your magnetic message to your prime target audiences.

Choose Your Words

Selecting the right words gets your story across and puts you in the driver's seat. Words are powerful symbols that help you take charge of your interview. Choose them wisely. Here is some intelligence to point you in the right direction:

- **Stay positive.** Tell your audience first what you will do, not what you hope to avoid.
- **Remain concise.** Brevity equals quotability. You may get but one six- to 10-second quote – or less – in the article or broadcast piece.
- **Prepare responses for routine questions.** There are certain topics nearly every reporter will cover. Be ready for them and know which part of your message best addresses each one.
- **Steel yourself for hot button issues.** Write down the hardball questions you most dread, and rehearse how you will use your message to respond.
- **Know when to say when.** Stop talking when you are finished with your answer and wait for the next question. Rambling aimlessly spells trouble.

CHAPTER 3

Walk a Mile in the Reporter's Shoes

The more you understand the rigors of a reporter's job, the better the chance your business deal will succeed. Once you forge a civil, professional relationship, the reporter will learn that you are a trusted source who can give them the reliable information and concise quotes they need.

As a former reporter, I realize that a walk through a journalist's mind can be a scary proposition. Still, let's take a quick tour.

Get to the Point

A reporter's thought process dictates that you cut right to the chase. Reporters want your headline first, then your lead paragraph, then the rich filling of examples, numbers, third-party support, and so forth. This style of communication is the polar opposite of our everyday conversations in which we build our case and gradually end with the crescendo. So it is important that you muster the discipline to think headline, lead paragraph (or "lede" as it's known in the trade), and support material in that order.

Consider this viewpoint as you construct your message, too, ensuring that it makes sense for the reporter and the public. Take a tip from this former reporter – journalists don't care when your company was established or how long it took your project to come to fruition. They want the grabber first.

It is up to you to visualize a vivid headline – think click bait; what is it that leads you to read a story online – and conjure up an ideal lead paragraph. Then and only then is the reporter ready to absorb the facts and figures that best support your message.

Journalists sometimes ask the "wrong" questions because they don't know the subject matter as well as you do. If you want your quotable quotes in the newspaper and on the cable news channels, it is up to you to make it easy for the reporter to understand your message by turning those wrong questions into the right answers.

You can also help reporters by taking into account the obstacles they face and helping them overcome them whenever appropriate:

- Unforgiving deadlines.
- Multiple assignments, often working on diverse stories simultaneously.
- Competitive pressures from other newspapers, magazines, radio and television stations, and blogs.
- Negative attitude of some sources.
- Professional pride and status; they want to impress their editors, news directors, and peers.
- Gruff and demanding editors and news directors.
- Fact checkers peering over their shoulders.
- Headline writers who may never read their entire article.

Most news sources never stop to think about how they can facilitate matters from the reporter's point of view. You gain an advantage when you do so.

Tricks of the Reporter's Trade

Reporters will be grateful if you prove helpful. But it is naïve to suggest there is not another side to this story. They thrive on conflict. After all, that is what sells newspapers, garners TV ratings points, and generates clicks.

Journalists have ways of trying to elicit information you may not want to cough up. Let us review some tricks of the reporter's trade you need to know about:

- **Planting words in your mouth**: Don't assume ownership of a reporter's loaded language. Keep it positive and answer in your own words.

- **Rapid fire questions**: When a reporter hits you with three or four questions in quick succession, choose the query that speaks to your message most seamlessly.

- **Interruption**: When a reporter cuts you short mid-thought, wait for the interruption to subside and remain of good cheer. Then finish your answer.

- **Hostile**: When things turn nasty, you must remain calm and polite. This is a business deal, not a personal vendetta.

- **Friendly**: Keep your guard up. Your aim is to cultivate reporters as business contacts, not to make friends.

- **What if**: Stick with what you know and keep hypotheticals out of the equation. It is not your job to gaze into a crystal ball.

- **Pause**: When you finish your reply and a silence hangs in the air, let the reporter fill it.

- **Columbo**: The interview seems about to conclude but the reporter, like the classic TV detective, says, "Oh, just one more thing ... " Beware this final trap.

Different reporters use different methods. By staying on the alert, you minimize your odds of uttering a quote that will come back to haunt you.

Ground Rules

Unless your duties dictate that you deal with reporters daily, you should always stay on the record. This is by far the safest and least confusing way to proceed. On the record means that the reporter can use anything involved in your business deal – the words you say, the materials you give them, hallway chatter in your office, even the gestures you make.

Leave the complex negotiations about going off the record or on background to your communications experts. They should know how to manage those delicate negotiations. We will delve into the specific meanings of each term later.

Rights and Responsibilities

To be sure, you have certain rights when you deal with the press. Among them:

- Right to know the subject of the interview and inquire what questions the reporter plans to ask.
- Right to set time limits in advance of the interview.
- Right to ask clarifying questions.
- Right to apply the ground rules to which you and the reporter agreed.
- Right to ask who else the reporter is interviewing.
- Right to record the interview for your records.

It's best to let your media relations staff obtain this information prior to any interviews. This removes C-suite executives and other spokespeople from the negotiations, allowing them to take on the mantle of the expert who remains above the fray. Plus, your staff person can play the "heavy" if needed; for example, if the reporter tries to extend the interview beyond your agreed upon time frame.

As with any relationship, with rights come responsibilities. You owe reporters the following as part and parcel of your business deal:

- Be honest.
- Say you don't know rather than guess at an answer.
- Respond in a timely manner.
- Learn about the reporter and the media outlet for which they work.
- Maintain a sense of professionalism at all times.

Keep these obligations in mind before you agree to any media interview.

CHAPTER 4

Interview Formats and How to Manage Them

You are likely to encounter multiple interview formats in your dealings with the press. Each has special wrinkles, so let's get specific and offer insider guidelines into some of the more common types.

Don't forget our old friend Practice! Practice! Practice when it comes to last-minute preparations. Verbalize your message at least once in private before you hit the airwaves or get on the phone. This helps you get your brain in gear and stay more focused.

Pencil and Paper Interviews

This in-person exchange may be the most common of any format. The reporter pulls out a notepad, asks you questions, and takes notes. They may also record the interview; you have the same right. How can you best prepare and perform?

- ✓ To the extent you are able, dictate where the meeting takes place. Do you want to confer in your office? Or is there too much chance of them seeing or hearing something inadvertently?
- ✓ Keep everything of a sensitive nature well out of sight. You don't want to beg any questions they may not have thought of previously.
- ✓ Maintain rock solid eye contact the whole time. Right or wrong, it adds to your credibility.

✓ Watch out for the charm offensive trap. When you start hearing how smart you are or how much they love your wardrobe, alarm bells should sound in your head.

✓ Stay on guard throughout. You may start to feel relaxed after a few minutes. While you may get into a groove with regard to delivering your message, do not allow yourself to get too comfortable.

✓ Whenever possible, a media relations staffer should accompany your C-suite leader or issue expert. They can step in – gently – if needed and take care of any follow up.

✓ The interview concludes when you and the reporter are out of sight and earshot. Don't fall for the old trick in which they close up the notepad and engage in seemingly small talk. It may be an attempt to coax you into saying something you will regret.

Telephone Interviews

Here are some special considerations to take into account when you are interviewed over the telephone by a print or radio reporter. Indeed, many of these points apply to nearly any interview format:

✓ When a reporter calls you, always call them back. Never launch into an interview on the spur of the moment. You need time to organize your thoughts and consider what message you want to convey.

✓ Ask what specific topic they want you to talk about.

✓ Determine their deadline.

✓ Find out who else they have interviewed. You need to learn, for instance, whether they have already talked with your adversaries and absorbed an opposing point of view.

✓ Write down the reporter's name and the media outlet for which they work and keep it in front of you so you know who you are talking to and where they are from.

✓ Print out and keep in your line of vision the four legs of your message in case you should falter.

✓ Shut down your computer and silence your mobile devices to eliminate distractions.

✓ Stand up during your interview, or at least sit up straight. Slouching reduces your energy level and weakens your voice.

✓ Remain alert throughout, as you would in any business deal. It's too easy to feel relaxed when on the phone.

Live Television

If you are interviewed as part of an in-studio television program, here are some basics to keep in mind:

✓ Arrive early so you can soak up the environment and get accustomed to it.

✓ Greet your host and producer. Don't expect that they will have a lot of time to talk with you, but do take a few moments if time allows to steer them toward the areas you want to cover.

✓ Avoid the green room and its buffet. You are there to work, not to eat.

✓ Chat up the guest before you. Was the host easy to work with or were they having a bad day?

✓ Check your look in a mirror.

✓ Once you are seated for your interview, ask for a shot in the monitor to see how you will look on TV.

✓ Always assume that the microphone is "hot" allowing everyone in the control room to hear and record you.

✓ Take in a few deep breaths just before the camera's tell light goes red.

✓ During the interview, maintain eye contact with your host. Ignore the cameras.

Radio Talk Shows and Podcasts

Radio talk shows and podcasts present one of the best opportunities to get your message out to specific, segmented audiences. Here's what to do when the "On the Air" light clicks on:

- ✓ Repeat your message numerous times, even during a short interview. Audiences tend to listen actively for only short bursts of time.
- ✓ Use notes if you like, but remember to keep them concise.
- ✓ Write your notes on index cards; they make less noise than paper.
- ✓ Write out the call letters of the station or the name of the podcast and the name of your interviewer; keep it visible for easy reference.
- ✓ Ask the host how close to the microphone you should sit. Every microphone and studio set up is different.
- ✓ Leave your listeners with a phone number, website, digital media handle, or email address where they can contact you for more information (a good idea for any interview format).

Be alert to the plethora of podcasts that may pursue you as a guest. These are not radio stations. They are often vanity projects launched by self-proclaimed gurus. If you determine that they reach your audience, great. But it is important to recognize that they differ significantly from over-the-air broadcasters (many of which do indeed stream their programming online in addition to broadcasting it over the airwaves).

Satellite Media Tours

The time may come when you sit in a studio and talk to a series of TV news anchors in far-flung cities via satellite. This is known as a satellite media tour (SMT). You may be talking to dozens of stations in rapid succession during a single half-day sitting. You may also find some radio interviews interspersed. Make use of the following strategies when participating in this type of discussion:

- ✓ Look into the camera. This is one of the rare times you should look straight at the camera lens since, in this instance, it takes the place of your interviewer.

- ✓ Realize that you will be using an earpiece – known as an IFB –to hear your questioner.
- ✓ Focus on your message; allow the technicians to deal with all the equipment.
- ✓ Write out the name of the city you are speaking to for every interview, and keep it in plain sight.
- ✓ Don't force it, but do use anecdotes and examples that are appropriate to specific cities.
- ✓ Keep your messages short and succinct; you won't have time to state more than two or three high-level points.
- ✓ You will get bored saying essentially the same thing 10 or 20 times. Bear in mind that each exchange reaches a new audience, one that has not heard from you before. Interview number 20 deserves the same amount of energy and enthusiasm as interview number one.
- ✓ Monitor your energy level. In fact, ask a colleague to keep an eye on this for you.

Skype or Zoom Interviews

Interviews conducted over video conferencing services were becoming trendier. Then the coronavirus pandemic hit and their frequency, well, zoomed up.

Who knows? A couple of years from now we could be back to holding interviews much as we have done in the past. That's my guess, and it is only a guess. It may not hold true if we experience another pandemic or a calamity of a different sort.

For all we know, the media could decide to stick with Zoom interviews for the foreseeable future. I can see two reasons for this. One, they assume the audience has gotten accustomed to the inferior quality and will live with it. Two, the seemingly never-ending – and debilitating – corporate cost cutting efforts make such interviews an attractive long-term option.

Keep these guidelines in mind when talking to reporters through your computer or mobile device:

- ✓ If you are not familiar with the technology, practice with a colleague or friend beforehand to iron out any kinks.
- ✓ Sign on early in case you need a bit of time to sort out any technical glitches.
- ✓ As with SMTs, keep your messages streamlined since you are likely to have limited time.
- ✓ Invest in an HD camera and a dedicated microphone. The microphones that come with your computer's camera are getting better, but still can suffer from low quality.
- ✓ Look into the camera lens. Too many interviewees stare at themselves or the reporter on the monitor, skewing their eye contact and diminishing the connection with viewers. As with SMTs, that lens assumes the role of your interviewer.
- ✓ Position your camera so that it is level with your eyes. Set your monitor, laptop, or tablet on a stack of books if need be. No one wants a view up your nose.
- ✓ Lighting is important. Avoid glaring bare bulbs that make you look ghostly. And don't keep things too dark. Place a soft light in front of you and, when possible, a soft backlight on the floor behind you. Ring lights work well, as do diffused LED lights on a collapsible tripod.
- ✓ Aim for an attractive, professional looking background. Green screens can work if you have a physical backdrop. Take a pass on those virtual backgrounds offered by services like Zoom. The technology isn't nearly as good, making it too easy for you to merge into the background with comical results.
- ✓ Do not sit in front of windows. The glare during daylight hours leaves you looking like a dark shadow. Plus, the dazzling brightness proves taxing to viewers.
- ✓ Similarly, do not sit in front of a mirror. Activity across the room or elsewhere in your house could be clearly visible.

✓ Dress and groom like a grownup. I never fail to be impressed by people who wear suits when on television even when interviewed from home. Mussed hair and ratty t-shirts are no-nos. Business attire, a shave, and makeup convey a professional look and feel.

✓ Keep kids, dogs, etc., at bay throughout.

✓ Inform family members when you plan to participate in a video call so they can avoid hollering across the house, traipsing across the background, etc.

No matter the format, be prepared for the reporter who asks whether they missed anything or if you want to add a final thought. You will not hear this question every time, but when you do, you've struck gold. This gives you a wide open opportunity to conclude your business deal one of two ways: 1) Restate briefly the essence of your message, emphasizing the leg of your message that best reaches the target audience for this media outlet and 2) if you have forgotten to mention one of your main message points, you've just been gifted a second chance.

Once your interview has ended, don't hesitate to pat yourself on the back for a job well done.

CHAPTER 5

Hot 100+ Media Tips

There is a lot to corral when dealing with the press. You can't always win the gold medal in the rodeo. In the real world, you don't always get a smooth ride.

Priorities become confused. Companies place tactics before strategy. Some interviewees prove incapable. Messaging efforts bog down when everyone tries to micromanage the process.

We have already covered a lot of ground. In this chapter, I will pull everything together and delve in greater detail into what has been offered so far. Follow these guidelines and you will be well on your way to transforming your media relations plow horse into a thoroughbred.

For instance, is more attention to your interview preparation process warranted? Does your messaging method need a shot in the arm? Could you use some advice about responding to questions? Perhaps you need to bolster your media relations shop. It's all here – the advice you need to organize a shipshape media outreach strategy, chart your course, and implement the right tactics capable of bringing that plan to life.

For your convenience, these hot 100+ tips are broken out into categories that reflect the issues you need to consider when engaging in your business deals with the media.

As noted earlier, it's a good idea to take lots of notes to highlight the recommendations on which you need to concentrate. Get your pen and paper or your tablet's keypad ready. Here we go.

Pre-interview Preparations

- **Practice, practice, practice** to prepare for every interview. This is by far the best way to sharpen your skills. In fact, it is one of the three pillars of nearly every media training workshop. Engaging in simulated interviews is essential to becoming a media darling. It's important to understand that practice does not always need to be formal. For instance, an in-house communications staffer can catch the CEO walking down the hallway and toss a few questions their way. Spokespeople can take advantage of 10-minute gaps between meetings to rehearse delivery. Arrange a 20-minute phone call with your media strategy consultant to discuss how to handle pressing issues. The point is you don't need to block out hours and hours of the day for every practice session. Make a conscious effort to make the most of those small chunks of time that present themselves nearly every day.

- **Research the reporters** who cover your domain. Learn what beat they typically cover and how well they know the nuts and bolts. This gets back to the need for relationship building. Perform due diligence on those scribes who contact you for comment. Do they know their stuff? Are they new to the beat? How long have they been with their current media outlet? Are they fresh out of journalism school or wise owls? What clips of theirs – print, audio, or video – can you unearth? Do they have a reputation for laziness? Are their questions incisive? What particular methods do they use to try to elicit information you don't want to give up? Smart media relations operators seek out answers to questions like these to give their companies a leg up.

- **Ask questions of others** who have encountered the reporter before. Check in with colleagues at other companies and with the communications staff at the associations that represent you. What scuttlebutt can they offer about the newsperson in question? Is there a particular technique the reporter uses to try to squeeze information out of interviewees? Are they good listeners or are they too busy forming their next question (or, worse from an ethical perspective, touting their own opinions)?

- **Learn the different needs** of print vs. radio vs. television reporters. While all journalists want quotable quotes for their stories and digital media posts, realize that print reporters often seek a larger quantity of information since they generally have larger news holes to fill. Radio reporters these days need quick-hitting comments. Listen to your local commercial all-news radio station. Their actualities (those audio sound bites they glean from sources) continue to shrink in length, sometimes dwindling to two or three seconds. The exceptions are NPR affiliates that often report in more depth. TV reporters want action and visuals. An author's note from years of observation (this is going to offend some): Print reporters are inclined to have deeper knowledge about the affairs they cover, including your business, since they often specialize in a particular beat. Radio reporters, by and large, take the news and their duty to report it seriously, though they are usually driven by the breaking news of the day. Television reporters tend to fall at the bottom of the expertise pile. I know, I know. I've just offended a bunch of folks. Allow me to add the caveat that there are exceptions to every rule. Diligent print correspondents work alongside some duds. Airheaded TV anchors share the newsroom with solid, veteran journalists who know their community intimately. I'm just explaining the averages as I've witnessed them over the decades. Your experience may vary.

- **Never take a reporter's call or answer their email on the spur of the moment**. A lack of preparedness will get you into trouble every time. Take some time to center yourself, review your message, and practice answering a few questions. Determine what their deadline is and offer to call back. Most reporters will want to call you at the appointed hour in order to gain control; that's fine. But if they keep you waiting (sometimes because they're busy, sometimes in an effort to throw you off balance), all bets are off. If you agreed to a 10 a.m. interview and they don't call you until 10:10 a.m., you have likely moved on mentally to something else. As a result, you won't be as sharp as you were 10 minutes before. In this situation, assuming the interview is important enough to you and your business goals, you have three choices. One, put the reporter on hold for a minute or two while you refresh your memory. They kept you waiting. Turnabout is fair play. Two, reschedule the interview if the reporter's deadline and your calendar permit. Three, bag the conversation if it is not a critical media hit for you.

- **Prepare for today's digital media environment** by recognizing that some reporters may tweet or blog during your news conferences and other events. Don't let this annoy you. The assembled crowd is not ignoring you (well, not necessarily; sure, they could be texting the spouse about dinner plans; you never know). There is one annoying *Washington Post* columnist who writes passages of his blog at live events (he also asks lots of unnecessarily rude questions, but that's another matter). The fact is it's not like the old days when reporters paid rapt attention and scribbled notes. Adjust to today's methods of news gathering.

- **Respond in a timely manner** to reporters' inquiries. Don't expect to have your viewpoint included if you respond at the last minute. Deadlines are sacrosanct in journalism. One of the easiest ways to get removed from a reporter's list of sources is to reply late or not at all. How can you determine the deadline? Ask. Every time. This is one piece of information the normally tight-lipped scribe tribe will readily share with you. If you cannot meet a deadline, let them know. Just because they have a time constraint doesn't mean you have one, necessarily.

- **Sort the questions you may face into three baskets**. The first basket contains the "friendlies." These are questions you want to hear; the ones you have fed the reporter beforehand. Basket number two is full of the routine queries you can anticipate hearing in nearly every interview: Tell me about your new product. Why are you working with Senator X on your public policy proposal? How does your new widget work? What makes it better than the competition's? The third basket contains questions you do not want to hear. They may be hostile or off-point. Regardless, you must be ready to confront them. Techniques like bridging help with the contents of basket three. Why do I recommend dividing questions into these three baskets? It clears the clutter from your brain during media exchanges. Rather than trying to keep a handle on a dizzying array of granular issues, you just need to sort your response into one of the three baskets. There, that takes some of the pressure off, doesn't it?

- **Anticipate and prepare for routine questions** you should expect in nearly every interview. Too often, basket number two is where people get tripped up. I witnessed an online session in which the president of an association took questions from his members. This happened during the coronavirus crisis. The questions were in writing and most were submitted in advance, so you would think responding would be fairly straightforward. A few days prior, I had raised with him one of the issues that was bound to be broached: During a time of reduced services, didn't members deserve some type of break on their dues? In the broadcast, he totally fumbled. His speech pattern, which had heretofore been superb, devolved into a series of disfluencies and uncomfortable pauses. His eye contact with the camera, which had been rock solid, dissolved, with his eyes seemingly searching for an answer somewhere in the ether. Lucky for him, no follow up was possible due to the format. Journalists would not have been so accommodating. He blew a golden opportunity to explain the organization's position. I believe it highly unlikely he persuaded many members that they should continue paying the same rate.

- **Conduct "The Third Degree" when preparing for a crisis**

situation. Put yourself behind a table or on a podium in the front of a room with TV lights shining in your eyes and have colleagues toss barbed inquiries during your media training workshop. Be sure to throw in some hardballs. I recommend bringing in the office skeptic as one of the inquisitors. Pair them with one or two of your communications executives (no toadies allowed) and your media strategy and training consultant. This group tends not to shy away from challenging authority figures, and will not accept feeble answers. They will push things to the limit. This is what you need. It is far better to see how responses hit the mark in a rehearsal session than under pressure from a quick-witted reporter. You may sometimes hear this called a "murder board" (a phrase originating, as best I can determine, with the military). I shun that term as too confrontational and inaccurate. You are not preparing to be slain. You are preparing to claim victory in a battle of wits.

- **Video record all of your formal media training exercises**. Critique the video immediately afterward, and invite your chief communications officer and media strategy consultant to do the same. Replaying and appraising your simulated interviews is, in my observation of more than 20 years, by far the most effective learning tool there is. It shows you in no uncertain terms where your communications strengths and challenges reside. Some participants report that watching themselves can be painful. It is often due to the fact that they have never seen themselves on video in a formal situation like this. Rest assured, this discomfort will diminish the more you see yourself. And don't let that video gather dust on an electronic shelf afterward. Turn back to it in the weeks and months ahead to gauge your improvement. It can be a valuable learning tool.

- **Limit the contents of your press kit to the essentials**. Among the items you can include are your news release, any pertinent news advisories, concise position statements, brief biographical sketches of your executives who are the faces and voices of the issue at hand, their head shots, video clips of past coverage, B-roll footage, legislative and regulatory testimony, your digital media channels, contact information for your media relations staff, and links to your website containing the information listed above. Do not overload reporters with extraneous material. Make conscious choices about what to exclude as well as include.

Priming the Reporter

- **Target your media opportunities**. Start by defining your target audience. Do you need to reach clients or prospects? Your Congressional delegation? Regulatory officials? People in a specific geographical area? Your workforce? Competitors? Determine which media outlets best reach your intended targets. The media is nothing more than a conduit that helps you reach out to your public. Reporters are not your ultimate audience. There are only so many hours in the day, so prioritize methodically. In most cases, you'll want to reach out to the biggest media bang first.

- **Forge professional relationships with reporters over time**. Only then can you build the trust that makes you a reliable source. Admittedly, this is getting harder to do in the era of shrinking newsrooms. Many reporters don't have time to sit down and chat over coffee for a "getting to know you" session. This creates a challenge when trying to figure out how to reach the media. What can you do? Don't waste a reporter's time. Avoid sending them news releases about your just hired vice president of happiness; they don't care. Reach out when you have real news: A breakthrough drug coming out of clinical trials, a response to a crisis, or a new public policy stance, for example. Get on their radar in a productive way. Eventually, they may learn to contact you when necessary. No guarantees. As I tell my clients, we are trying to raise the odds for success. Any counselor who pledges victory is promising more than they can deliver.

- **Supply the reporter with background information** about your company and your issue ahead of time. This can include news releases, web links, fact sheets, speeches, digital media channels, and more. The more you furnish up front, the less time you'll need to waste during those precious interview minutes. You may want to briefly reinforce some of the basics when talking to the correspondent, but don't go dredging up the year your business was founded, your college ties, or the minutiae surrounding un-related issues. The reporter should be able to grab all of that from the package you supplied up front.

- **Send a list of frequently asked questions** you want them to raise. I have observed more than once a reporter go down the very collection I've presented to them. They may or may not turn to your promptings every time, but you at least raise the odds that they will inquire about those issues. And that's the goal of any media outreach effort, to raise your odds for success. No guaran-tees. But if I told you that I can raise your probability of success from zero to 75 percent, wouldn't you take that bet?

- **Ask the reporter who else they have talked to** for their story. It helps to know who else has provided context for them. Have they already interviewed your mortal enemy? Or have they focused on your allies? These insights give you valuable clues as to their attitude toward you and the type of questions they might ask – friendly, neutral, or hostile. Asking about this is one of the rights you have in your business deal with the media. They may or may not tell you this and other items such as the questions they plan to ask. Remember, we're in the business of raising your odds for success, so if you can get this information from half of the report-ers you deal with, you're raising your chances for triumph.

- **Approach each reporter with the notion that you have an opening** to make a new professional acquaintance, not a buddy.

Earlier, I wrote about the value of seeing every interview as an opportunity. Tattoo that word on your brain during your media dealings. Reporters seek you out as a source of information, not as a potential new friend. I'm not saying there is anything wrong with having reporters for friends. They are, by and large in my encounters, nice folks. Just remember that you are engaged in a business deal when they interview you for professional purposes, and that all the standard ground rules apply. You are, for example, always on the record whenever you encounter them – even in seemingly casual situations – unless both of you explicitly agree otherwise.

- **Aim to understand what a reporter's day is like**. The more you can place yourself in their shoes, the better you can give them what they need – on your terms, of course. For instance, their routine is replete with unforgiving deadlines. Get a sense of their timing needs. Do they need to talk with you by close of business today or can it wait until next week? Today's newsrooms also face increasingly tight budgets. They have neither the luxury of time nor of infinite resources. Take, for example, the community of regional reporters based in our nation's capital. Many used to work out of offices in the National Press Building. Several years ago, media outlets started shuttering those offices, making the reporters work from home. Next, many closed the bureaus altogether, throwing journalists out of work. If you deal with reporters who have fewer newsroom colleagues, you are likely facing someone dealing with high anxiety. Those sources who make their jobs easier are likely to be turned to often. They have less time to dig into context, so offer background information that explains your contention in a concise manner. Correspondents may have to report to their cranky editor and news director bosses. Look, we all know what it's like to work under a cretin. Give your reporters a story that's going to make them look good to their superiors. This way, you can better help them tell your story.

- **Take into account the fact that reporters are always working.** You remain on the record even during an after hours, seemingly casual chat. You do not have license to spill the beans about confidential or sensitive issues when you bump into a member of the media at a conference or reception (or in the neighborhood if you happen to live next door to one). It is their job to vacuum up juicy tidbits wherever and whenever they find them. Any time you are in the presence of a reporter, your radar should be pulsing at full intensity.

Sharpen Your Mindset

- **Think of every media interview as a business deal.** This is one of the primary lessons I try to instill in my clients. It's no different than going to the grocery store and buying a gallon of milk. The store has something you want – the milk. In exchange, you give the store your money. When dealing with the press, you have something the reporter wants – information, ideally in the form of a juicy, message-driven quote – in exchange for spreading your message. No, this does not involve an exchange of money (in some cultures, maybe, but in the United States, that is highly unethical). Bear in mind at all times that you are involved in a business deal no matter whether the reporter is your friend or how chummy they seem. Let me emphasize one more time: It's a business deal. And given the reach of the media, it is among the most important business deals you will ever conduct.
- **Let opportunity be your watchword.** Some spokespeople undertake media interviews with trepidation. I see it all the time in media strategy and training workshops, especially among those with less experience. Yet it lingers among some old hands, too. While caution is warranted, viewing this as a threat is unproductive. The media is not necessarily your enemy. In fact, a huge percentage of your interactions will prove to be straightforward and

informational in nature. Any interview could be the big break your business needs, putting you closer to reaching your most critical business and public policy goals. These are two of the most important media relations keys you can take in: **Business deal** and **opportunity**.

- **Why is the reporter contacting you** to begin with? Ponder why you were approached for an interview in the first place. What is it about your public profile or your opinion on the issue that makes you stand out from the crowd? How can you map out what potential issues you want to take the initiative to promote and those you want to reactively respond to? Considering this line of thought can add to your depth of understanding just what the reporter is looking for.

- **Remain honest at all times**. If you lie, you lose your credibility, and your days as a news source are done. Nothing burns a source faster and more completely than dishonesty. While an interview is not akin to a courtroom where you have to tell "the truth, the whole truth, and nothing but the truth," two of those principles remain. Anything you say must be the truth to the best of your knowledge. If it is not something you know about, you shouldn't be commenting on it. In addition, whatever you say must be nothing but the truth, no lies allowed. As for spilling the whole truth, you are not required to do so with the press. You have a message to deliver. Not every factoid fits into that message. If a reporter fails to ask you about something, you are under no obligation to spill the beans. If they do raise sensitive issues, you need to develop the ability to acknowledge the question, then quickly bridge back to your message. This is not a legal proceeding. Say what you're there to say being faithful to the facts. Stay honest on your terms.

- **Don't even think about picking a fight** with someone who owns a printing press or gobbles bandwidth by the terabyte. Oh, it may feel good to give it to that reporter who consistently gets things wrong or mischaracterizes your point of view. But you are not going to win in the final analysis. If they get something wrong, you have the right to ask them to correct the record. When you do so, be firm but be respectful. Beating them up like a bullying New York City developer rarely works. Whether you like it or not, they – not you – have the last word.

- **Be true to your own style**. I hear it all the time: I want to mimic the Dalai Lama, Steve Jobs, or Michelle Obama (or insert your favorite public figure here). Forget it. The odds are slim that you will ascend to those heights. You are you, so work with what you've got. Play to your own communications strengths and work to improve or alleviate your challenges. Sure, observe those you admire, but don't strive to become them. You will only come across as a phony. The bottom line: Learn from others, but don't try to slip into their shoes.

- **Maintain your professionalism**. Some reporters will try to get under your skin. And some are pretty good at it, having practiced for years. Let them try. Your sole goal is to deliver your message in a compelling manner that raises the odds for its inclusion in the reporter's story. You are not there to make a best friend forever or a mortal enemy. Your ambition is to further your company's business or public policy goals. When a reporter tries to ruffle your feathers, ignore the tactic and maintain your good grace and tact. Be the adult in the room. This is a must no matter how ruffled you feel.

- **You are the expert.** Keep that thought in the forefront of your mind. Otherwise, why would a reporter want to talk with you? Admittedly, this is a confidence building move for those times when your knees knock and voice quivers. At the same time, it must be true. Why would your company put you front and center under the white hot lights of the media unless you are capable of broadcasting a magnetic message? Reality check: Are there inept interviewees? You bet. But they tend to be weeded out pretty quick. One bad performance can sideline that individual forever, and rightly so. But assuming you buy in to the notion of sustained professional development, that laggard is not you, is it?

- **Shun that old ruse of claiming a reporter took your words "out of context."** This is a sure sign of an amateur media source at work. I can only shake my head and roll my eyes when I hear someone make this claim. It's nothing more than a ham-handed attempt to walk back something they wish they hadn't said. You, not the reporter, are responsible for your comments. If you said it, you own it. Plain and simple.

- **Refuse to spread the notion of "fake news."** This is a refuge of scoundrels and unhinged conspiracy theorists. Do the media get things wrong on occasion? Of course, don't we all. Are some reporters more fair and diligent than others? You bet. Nonetheless, there are "media" organizations that trade in rumors they know to be false. In my view, they do not qualify as media outlets and you are best off not to deal with them (if you are one of those unprincipled rumor-mongers and you are reading this: First of all, I'm amazed you made it this far; second, please go away).

- **Maintain a positive attitude**. Along with messaging and technique, your outlook goes a long way toward determining the success of your media campaign. Those who enter into the business deal thinking that reporters are a bunch of aimless hacks are likely to experience poor outcomes. On the positive side, those who view interacting with the press as an opportunity are likely to show superior results. An enhanced reputation. More confidence in the public arena. Career advancement. Achievement of key business and public policy goals. Magnetic messages. Sparkling spokespeople. Those are your objectives.

Formats for Your Business Deals with the Media

- **Study the difference between live and taped interviews** when approached by the electronic media. Here are the distinctions: 1) Live interviews: You're talking in real time. There are no edits, no do-overs. Some executives feel pressured, believing this is a disadvantage. I disagree. Live interviews give you and your message a clear, unobstructed runway. 2) Taped or recorded interviews: No one actually uses tape anymore, but the lingo lingers. This format is likely to be edited for length or to fit your comments into a larger package that includes other viewpoints. The reporter or producer will excerpt the juiciest bites you put forward, which makes it imperative that you stay on message throughout the interview. No detours. No concessions to the other side. You don't want them lifting a segment that puts you in a negative light. For my money, taped interviews are where the pressure really comes into play. 3) Live to tape interviews: These are typically longer unedited pieces that are recorded for later playback. Think of a podcast or a 30-minute public affairs program. For instance, when I conduct audio interviews for C-suite Blueprint Radio, I tell my guests that it will be live to tape so they do not expect me to edit their words at all.

- **Arrive early for an in-studio television interview**. Get accustomed to your environment. Get into the studio early if you can, stand in an out-of-the-way nook and observe. Watch how they shuttle guests in and out and be alert to your host's mannerisms. If you get a chance, ask other guests about the host's approach. Don't expect time for a chitchat with your interviewer, especially if yours is a live shot. They are busy segueing from story to story and have plenty on their mind. Odds are you will be met by a producer. Never ignore these people. They are the ones who run the show. While the anchors get all the face time, the producers are the ones who book guests. Take a few moments to establish a relationship with your producer. Understand that they also do not have all the time in the world. However, a big part of their job is to secure guests and make them feel more comfortable (unless you know ahead of time that you're in for a confrontational grilling).

- **Refuse to be charmed by the green room.** This is the area backstage where TV guests cool their heels while waiting to hit the bright lights. I suggest avoiding the green room altogether whenever possible. There is little to learn there. They will try to tempt you with coffee and bagels. Ignore the refreshments. You're not there to nosh. You're there to impart an important message to the viewing public. Plus, eating just before you go on can dull your senses and slow your reaction time. As recommended above, get into the studio as soon as possible to get a feel for your interview location. I'll allow two exceptions to this green room rule: First, if the producer leads you in there and denies your request to enter the studio; you've got to respect that wish if they insist. Second, if you know there is another guest in the green room that you want some face time with. This could be anyone from an expert you have not yet met who supports your cause to your favorite author you just think it would be cool to meet.

- **Check your look in a mirror** before you enter the studio. The green room probably has a mirror (though again, you don't want to spend much, if any, time there) as will the restroom. What if you're not able to hit the loo beforehand? Pull out your phone and use the front-facing camera. Is there a stray hair you need to tend to? Any spinach in your teeth from that breakfast omelet? Has your lipstick become smeared? Is your tie straight and knotted properly? Your appearance counts. Think of how many times you've watched a televised discussion only to be distracted by an unkempt shirt collar or clown-like makeup. The memory burned into that brain of yours is more likely to be of that fashion faux pas than what that individual said. You don't want to give those viewers at home any reason to neglect your message.

- **Let the technicians do their job** of getting you seated, placing the microphone in its proper position, and arranging the lights.

They are the pros who can help you look and sound good. On the flip side, they can also make you look and sound terrible. If you come across as rude, maybe the shot will just happen to accentuate that glare from your forehead or put your volume level just a tad too low. They may use a wired or wireless lavaliere microphone. These are the small units that clip to your shirt, jacket, or tie. Be aware that, if wired, they may want to run the cord up your sleeve or the front of your blouse. Don't be offended. They are only trying to make you look and sound as natural as possible. They have done this a million times before and will do everything possible to ensure your comfort.

- **Find a comfortable seated position** for your interview. You are apt to have at least a few seconds to settle in. Use that time wisely. I recommend a "starting line" posture. Place one foot squarely on the floor in front of you. The other foot curls underneath your chair. Your rear end occupies the front edge of the chair. This helps you look – and feel – willing and open. It also opens up your upper body's nonverbal possibilities. For instance, you can use hand gestures more readily and lean forward to lend an air of excitement. Once you're settled, maintain your pose for the duration. This is not to say you should morph into a statue, but don't shift or squirm; you'll appear nervous and untrustworthy.

- **Ask the director or floor manager for a "shot"** on a monitor. What does this mean? You check yourself out on one of the floor monitors to get an idea how you will look on TV. This allows you to make any last-minute adjustments. Realize that getting a shot will not be possible in every situation. The studio may not have a monitor they can turn in your direction or they may be stretched for time. Regardless, it never hurts to ask.

- **Look at your interviewer** during a TV interview. Maintain eye contact with them throughout and ignore the cameras. We've all witnessed on-camera guests who look furtive because they don't know where to aim their gaze. They start with the host, cast a sideways glance into the camera, sneak a peek at their notes, then check the monitor. It looks unprofessional and shifty-eyed. Experienced sources lock in eye contact with their interviewer. Are there exceptions? Of course. If, for example, you are demonstrating a product or displaying a visual prop of some sort, you'll want to look in that direction as a means of cueing the viewers to look there, too. Once you've made that point, turn back to the host right away.

- **All of these principles also apply to a satellite media tour (SMT).** In this case, you sit in a remote location and participate in a round of interviews with several faraway stations consecutively. You listen to your interviewer through an earpiece known as an IFB. The camera substitutes for the reporter's eyes, so this is one of the few times you need to look directly into the camera. This speaks to two situations. Be aware that this is often an exhausting experience, sitting in a tiny studio and delivering the same basic message (throwing in a specific or two tailored to each local market) time and again. You really need to fortify your message discipline for this format.

- **A video interview on a service such as Skype or Zoom** represents the other time you should sustain eye contact with the camera. To look like a real media pro, maintain your eye contact with the camera lens of your computer or mobile device, not your screen. Why does the eye contact of so many interview subjects appear off kilter during remote video interviews? They are looking at their monitor, not the camera, which is typically slightly above the screen. Look at the camera lens during offsite interviews. If you plan to do such interviews frequently, invest in a good microphone. The superior sound quality is worth it.

- **Remember that the interview begins** as soon as you open your car door or as soon as the reporter enters your office building. Everything that anyone in your company says and does is on the record. Overheard hallway chatter? Fair game for the press.

A quick glance at a confidential slide through the glass wall of your conference room? That's legitimate news for the next day's edition (and, more immediately, its website). Strolling into the studio for a TV interview? If that last-minute prep session between media relations staffer and CEO is overheard, that can be characterized on air. Turn off your mobile devices and computer monitor to make sure no sensitive documents or awkward alerts from co-workers pop up. Alert your office mates to a reporter's presence. Chatter in the break room about the boss' peccadillos is fair game if the reporter overhears it. Bear in mind the old Navy adage "Loose lips sink ships." Don't torpedo your own efforts.

- **Keep in mind that the interview ends** when your car door closes or when the reporter exits your building. Don't let slip any inadvertent morsels as the elevator door is closing. One favorite technique of print scribes – known as the Columbo technique after the legendary TV detective – is to close the notebook and act as if the interview has concluded. Then they hit you with the "Oh, just one more question" routine. Don't let your guard down. You remain on the record. A similar trick used by the electronic media is to engage you in seemingly small talk while the technical crew packs up its gear. Here, too, refuse to fall for it. In either case, they may flatter you by saying how great the interview was (whether that is true or not) or may talk about something as mundane as the weather. Then they drop the bomb when you least expect it. To reiterate: This is a business deal. Keep it on that level until Elvis has left the building.

Magnetic Messaging

- **Build your magnetic message**. This takes time, patience, and care. The charge should be led by your communications staff since they are the ones who (theoretically) possess the necessary knowledge. If your staff is lacking in this department, engage a media strategy consultant. Get the key people in the room and hammer things out. For the first cut, include any issue experts. Draft your messaging document and circulate it for comment. Pull in the C-suite as you refine things. Messaging is typically not an exercise accomplished in an hour or two, so manage everyone's expectations and time accordingly.

- **Keep your messaging document to a single page**. Under no circumstances should this be a multi-page tome. Keep it to one sheet – your four main message points backed up by evidence that buttresses your viewpoint (more below on why four points is generally the magic number).

- **Think in terms of your headline first**. That's how a reporter's mind works. In today's journalistic environment, eyeballs matter since editors pay attention to online statistics, so feed the reporter a click bait-worthy line they can use. Cut to the chase right away. This sounds like a no-brainer, but it takes some work for this is not how most of us conduct everyday conversations. During a routine chat, we tend to start with some background, building up to a crescendo – our headline. That is not what reporters need, or what will serve you well when driving home your message. Reporters want the headline – the big, bold four- to eight-word neon sign that displays your message. Next, give them the lede (that's not a misspelling; for the story behind this journalistic jargon, see A Reporter's Glossary in Chapter Six). Think of the lede as the first sentence or two you would see in a newspaper article. Only then should you backfill your answers with the facts and figures that prove your point. Yes, you need that supporting material, but it should not be the heart of what you deliver. If you get nothing in that reporter's story other than your headline, that's still a victory, so deliver that header up front, then build the support structure for it. News sources who don't make the cut tend to be those who deliver a doctorate-level thesis to people who only want to know its title.

- **Build your magnetic message on four solid points**. Remember the analogy of these four points representing the legs of a sturdy chair. If just one of those legs proves wobbly, your message – and you – will collapse to the floor in no time.

- **Prove your message.** It's not enough to make a declarative pronouncement and leave it at that. You may come across to reporters as the world's most trustworthy person. No matter. You have to prove your perspective holds water. How? Serve up anecdotes, numbers, surveys, consumer testimonials, support from third parties, and other proof points that result in quotable quotes (as described in Chapter Two). Support each leg of your message with these proof points capable of resonating with the reporter.

- **Revisit your messaging regularly**. What does regularly mean? It depends. When you are in the midst of a full-blown crisis, you may need to update it hourly or even minute-by-minute in the early stages. For a low level, fairly static issue, every six months may suffice. Understand that messages are dynamic creatures requiring constant care and feeding. To ensure you check on them adequately, place a reminder on your calendar or task list.

Your Performance during the Business Deal

- **Stick to your message throughout your interview**. Return to it in response to every single question. This is not optional. Do not wander. Do not allow the reporter to lead you down the garden path; you may end up inside that dreaded last house on the left. A big part of your messaging efforts surrounds discipline – having the discipline to impart your stance in every question in every interview. Repeating the same words ad nauseum is tough and it feels unnatural. It is important to remember that the reporters – and, more important, their viewers, readers, and listeners – are hearing it for the first time. Consistency of message matters.

- **Use vivid language to ensure you speak in quotable quotes**.

Don't make reporters work hard to get your story in print and on the air. After all, you're the one who wants the ink; help them get it for you. You have so many tools at your disposal: Colorful stories, action verbs, comparisons, numbers, extremes, third-party endorsements, references to current events, famous quotes, and survey findings can be your friends. Decide which work best for your style and lean on them. If you really want to advance your profile as a spokesperson, choose one technique you don't feel comfortable using currently and work to make it a part of your repertoire. You may find that, over time, you'll acquire a new tool you can turn to.

- **Avoid talking in jargon**. Plain language is a virtue, even if you are talking with the wonkiest trade reporter. That reporter is, after all, merely a vehicle for delivering your message. Readers may not be familiar with your lingo. That jargon-laced soliloquy that you were so proud of will likely end up on the proverbial cutting room floor. The media outlet may use it for background, but the odds of it appearing in print credited to you are not high. A colleague once told me of a source she worked with who had in-depth, extended interviews with a well-known *New York Times* reporter. Yet the source was frustrated that she never got quoted in the newspaper. It turns out that her expertise was top notch, but her language so dense it was unquotable for a general circulation daily. Once the reporter had her information in hand, he turned to others who knew how to structure quotes about the issue. Your primary purpose is not to educate reporters; it is to get you and your company's point of view into the public eye.

- **Never, ever say "no comment."** You might as well wave a red cape in a bull ring. There will be times when you are legitimately unable to comment on an issue. This happens most typically when it revolves around an ongoing legal or personnel matter, or when proprietary issues come into play. However, "No comment" is not the way to deal with such situations. Instead, tell the reporter why you cannot delve into the issue because, for instance, you do not comment on pending legal cases. Professional members of the Fourth Estate will understand. Still, it is wise to stay on guard as they may try to come back for another bite later in the interview. When that happens, calmly explain again why you cannot comment, then – as with every response – move back to your message.

- **Emphasize the positive** throughout your interview. Steer clear of negative language. Reporters learn to be cagey about how they pose questions. One of the ways they do this is by trying to plant the negative in your mouth. They may ask, "Why are your first quarter results so poor?" The knee-jerk reply is, "Our results were not that poor." Let's analyze this. In the reader's eyes, who just brought up the fact of poor financials? You did. In any format other than a live radio or television interview, the reporter's questions are rarely included, only your answers. How can you avoid negative language? Turn things around by ignoring the negative in the question. In our example above, you might say, "As a matter of fact, our quarterly results improved compared with last year's first quarter so, as I've noted, we are on the right track." Accentuate the positive.

- **Set time limits in advance** of your interview and enforce them. Stay away from overly long requests. Anything longer than 20 minutes gives you plenty of time for a few things, such as straying off message or opening the door to a sensitive issue you had not intended to divulge. If you can't get your message across in 20 minutes or less, you should not be dealing with the press. Make it clear to the reporter when arranging the question and answer session that you have 20 minutes (or 15, or 10, or five; it's your decision). As your interview winds down, enforce that agreement. The reporter may try to extend things, especially if they want something from you that you are not inclined to give. Note well: Media relations staffers should be the ones to set forth the ground rules and impose them to keep the expert spokesperson above the fray.

- **Come prepared with third-party references**. Basically, you want other credible sources to say nice things about you. These are contacts who agree to support you and your efforts. It could be a dispassionate expert in your field, a celebrity, your trade association (or, if you represent an association, one of your notable members), a think tank scholar, or any number of other independent voices. The key here is to line up these sources before you need them. Forge these relationships as a matter of course throughout your career, so that, when you need them, you don't need to chase them. By then, it's too late. You score bonus points if you get a routine opponent to bolster you when needed. An example: When I led the communications shop for an association, we took note of some supportive words from a U.S. senator who habitually bashed us. During one public policy skirmish, however, he lauded our stance. You can bet that, at every opportunity, we used his quotes to our advantage.

- **Control the flow during a news conference**. You choose who asks questions in what order. Refuse to let the horde take charge by screaming questions. Settle things down by calmly calling on questioners. Try to get a sense in advance which reporters will be in the room. Right after your initial remarks, decide who you will recognize first. You may opt for the individual who has been covering you the longest – the "dean" of your press contingent – or someone who is unlikely to toss a hardball your way. The point is you want to make this a conscious choice. If you find yourself besieged by challenging broadsides, call on a relatively friendly face. You may not get a total softball, especially if your issue is contentious. If, however, you can dial down the hostility quotient from 100 to 50, consider it a victory of sorts. As you get ready to wrap up your news conference, inform the assembled multitude that you have time for one or two more questions. This phrasing is important. If you can easily respond to the first one, do so, re-iterate the basics of your message, and stride from the podium. If the first query is a tough one, ask for one more question in hopes that it will be less edgy. As always, there are no guarantees this will be the case. Remember that, with all these techniques, our goal is to improve your odds for success with the press.

- **Do not allow your news conference to drag on endlessly.** Set your time limit and stick to it. Don't let any moans and groans from the scribe tribe knock you off your plans. Give yourself five minutes or so to set a baseline with some introductory comments, allow 10 to 20 minutes for questioning, conclude matters with a brief recitation of the essence of your message. Tell the crowd how they can get additional information – perhaps on your website – and who they should contact for follow up, then get out of there.

- **Assign one person the task of concluding your news conference.** A simple, "Thank you, ladies and gentlemen," sends a signal to the press that the session is over. Assign this to one of your media relations staff members. This takes the pressure off you. Two critical notes here. One, your staffer needs to have the chutzpah to holler out the closing "thank you" above the din of the crowd. Two, you need to accept this cue and bring the news conference to an end. It appears awkward and disorganized when your company representatives aren't on the same page. Discuss how to end the session during your preparations, and make sure everyone agrees to abide by it.

- **Use index cards if you bring notes** for an audio podcast or radio talk show interview. Why index cards? The microphones will pick up the rustling noise made by plain paper. One of the great benefits of audio interviews is your ability to reference concise notes. Having a written prompt can bring a sense of comfort. That said, do not show up with a 10-page detailed outline. That makes you look ill-informed. Jotting down your main messages and perhaps a word or two to remind you of a key fact you want to be sure to deliver or a story you want to tell should suffice. A reminder: Take any notes with you as you depart. After every media encounter, scan the area for any "incriminating evidence." You don't want to leave any internal intelligence in the hands of the press since your notes may contain some sensitive or confidential information that the media would love to report (and your competitors would love to discover.

- **Drink water during your interview**. I don't mean that you should chug a gallon or two. That will only necessitate trips to the restroom (or a clearly uncomfortable crossing of your legs and squirming in your seat, taking your concentration off the job at hand). A sip every so often to wet your whistle is fine. The best idea is to hydrate the day before an interview or series of interviews, especially for a potentially taxing satellite media tour. This should sufficiently prepare your body while avoiding the need to trot down the hall the day of your appearance. Why is water the beverage of choice? Coffee, tea, or juice dries your mouth, robbing your voice of its power. Stick with good old H2O.

- **Ignore all the hustle and bustle** if you do an in-studio radio or television interview. Keep your focus on delivering your message. You are likely to observe lots of furtiveness and running around that has absolutely nothing to do with you. Your host may be getting cues in their IFB (see Chapter Six to learn about the IFB) that you're not aware of. They may even be hearing these sweet nothings from their producer while talking to you. It's a skill that takes lots of practice not to get flummoxed since it's hard to say one thing while hearing another. Try it some time. You'll have newfound respect for news anchors. Bottom line: Let the station staff figure out what they need to figure out. Your only job is to impart your message. If something of a technical nature should go wrong, take your lead from the host. If they forge ahead, you do the same. If they should need to pause or restart, they will let you know. Be patient. Smile. Wait for the storm clouds to clear.

- **Remain flexible** on the day of your interview. Media outlets are constantly besieged by breaking news, so your appointment may be pushed back. Don't take this personally. The reason they call it "news" is because of its late breaking pattern (don't get me started on those ceaseless and now-meaningless television news bumpers that feature breathless reports from the "live desk" – just once I'd love to see that desk spring to life and scare the bejeezus out of the reporter – or that endlessly touted "breaking news"). Okay, now back to our regularly scheduled commentary. The media must often make spur-of-the-moment decisions on what to cover. If your planned interview is not immediately timely, you may find yourself bumped for anything from a presidential announcement to a three-alarm blaze. It happens. If the reporter is late, roll with it. If you need to reschedule, do so. And don't hold a grudge. That won't win you any friends or ample coverage.

- **Be alert to the fact that you are constantly subject to being recorded**. Not so long ago, it was hard to conceal a bulky video camera. Now we all walk around tethered to mobile devices that record both audio and video. Reporters have them, too, as do opponents who would love to get the drop on you. Wise executives are always "on" when in public. This includes those seemingly innocuous times when you are at restaurants, receptions, hallway conversations during conventions and conferences, waiting to cross the street, airplanes, airport lounges – in short, anywhere you are around other people, especially unfamiliar people. Where can you let your guard down? Basically, two places: Within the four walls of your office and once you get home.

Nonverbal Fundamentals

- **Your Audio Tools** represent the way you sound. They include such features as your pitch, articulation, volume, emotion, and rate. The importance of three of these tools in particular – pitch, volume, and rate – is that you vary them over the course of your interviews. For example, when making a crucial point, you might raise or lower the pitch of your voice to add extra emphasis. As for volume, many people think that talking louder is the way to go. While that can be effective, don't ignore the value of softening your speech. You may even succeed at making reporters inch forward in their seats when you do so. Your rate of speech is also relevant. Speed up for a sentence or two, then slow down. And don't underestimate the usefulness of an occasional pause. That momentary silence can really perk up a reporter's ears. These tactics serve to make you more interesting to listen to and, thereby, a more effective media source.

- **Your Video Tools** dictate the way you look. They consist of your actions, facial expressions, eye contact, wardrobe, and props. Action is a broad category encompassing everything from your position (i.e., seated vs. standing), hand gestures, head movements, leg jiggling (please don't), and more. The most pleasing facial expressing is, no surprise, the smile. Use it when appropriate. A frown, eyebrow raise, or furrow of the brow also qualify. Your eye contact with the reporter, particularly in televised interviews, should be rock solid. This does not feel natural to most of us, so be sure to practice keeping 100 percent eye contact during your practice rounds. Regarding wardrobe, as noted earlier, dress for success, like a professional. Props include anything you must physically handle in an interview. Decide when to bring it into play and, importantly, when to put it down; this latter movement is where many sources trip themselves up. Use your props when you rehearse. I delve into your Audio Tools and Video Tools in more detail in my book, *The Truth About Public Speaking: The Three Keys to Great Presentations*. Another excellent resource is Joe Navarro's book, *What Every Body Is Saying*.

- **Never become defensive**. Your defensiveness tells reporters they have struck a nerve. They will soon be circling for the kill. Some reporters are attuned to your nonverbal signals. If they hear your vocal pitch tighten a notch or two, see your nostrils flare, or notice you back away from them, they become curious. How can you avoid these behaviors? Admittedly, it's hard to control instinctive reactions. You can try to mitigate them by smiling (assuming you are not discussing a tragic situation) and breathing. You'd be surprised how many people forget the simple act of breathing properly when stressed. Since many of us freeze when confronted with danger, you can also ease some of the tension by moving ever so slightly – a quick and barely noticeable stretch of the fingers or a slight flex of your ankle. Also, pay attention to your shoulders. Under tense conditions, we may find our shoulders way up above our neck. Get those shoulders down into a more neutral position. Needless to say, your verbal behavior also matters. Displaying defensiveness by countering with "Why are you asking me that?" or "That's a fake news question" is unlikely to earn you esteem in the reporter's eyes. The rule of thumb I share with my clients: Don't open any doors you do not want the reporter to enter. Opening it even the tiniest of cracks allows reporters to kick it down and charge through, shining a spotlight on your embarrassing or painful issue. Do this and you will lose all control of the exchange, something you never want to cede.

- **Make sure your delivery is congruent**. A skilled reporter will also sense if you are sending conflicting audio and video signals, and will likely begin to probe for holes in your argument. If, for example, you tell a reporter how tragic it is that one of your prime competitors has gone into bankruptcy while saying it with a big smile, you can expect them to follow up with some challenging interrogatories. And we've all seen interviews with a source who says how happy and excited they are to be in the studio, while their tone of voice and seating position tell us something completely different. This is why recording your practice sessions on video is so crucial. If your nonverbals lack congruence, you'll spot it right away and can work to correct it before sitting down with the press.

- **Play to your strengths and minimize your challenges** when utilizing your Video Tools and Audio Tools. It never ceases to amaze me that, with all the research that has been done into how people learn, some consultants still walk into a strategic media training session with a 2x4, eager to whack participants over the head for even the most minor of slips. This is not how professionals learn. The first step, naturally, is to assess your strengths and challenges. To do this, jot down the Audio Tools and Video Tools you read about above. Next to each, indicate whether you believe it to be one of your strengths or challenges. Zero in on your strengths first for this is where your most rapid improvement will come. Assess how you can maintain or improve them. Only then should you turn to your challenges. Pick the one you'd like to improve first. Work on it over the coming weeks and months. Once you feel more comfortable with it, move on to the next challenge you want to conquer. Important note: Concentrate on only one challenge at a time. Overloading yourself results only in frustration and, ultimately, failure to improve.

- **Take into account that a journalist can characterize your actions** and environment as well as your words in their article. If they write about "The confident sounding executive" or "She firmly stated," you've hit the mark. On the other hand, "He said haltingly," or "She replied, taken aback," are not characterizations you want to see associated with your quotes.

- **Dress professionally.** I really shouldn't need to say this, but today's fashion sense being what it is, it merits a mention. If you're invited to appear on TV, dress like you care. Men, is it really too much to ask to wear a suit and tie? Women, how about a crisp business suit? Unless you are in the field at an oil rig or stocking grocery shelves, etc., display a professional wardrobe. This also pertains to remote interviews. No matter if you're broadcasting remotely from your bedroom, gin up a respectable background and don that executive wardrobe. It reinforces your credibility.

- **Stay away from herringbones** and tight checked patterns when appearing on TV. Viewers will spend more time talking about how your shirt or jacket visually breaks up (called "flaring") than they will listening to your message. Refuse to extend an invitation to distraction. Note that this advice also applies to video conference interviews and, in fact, video conferences in general. Stick with solid neutral colors and contrasts, for instance, a navy blue blazer with a light blue shirt or some such combination. This also applies to ties. You may dearly cherish that loud novelty tie your kids gave you for your birthday. Fine. Wear it proudly everywhere you want — just not on TV. Also think twice about lapel pins since they are typically too small to be discerned on the home viewer's screen. Bright multi-colored blouses can also prove distracting, as can reflective brooches, jangling bracelets, big flowers, and plunging necklines.

Q&A Strategies

- **Serve up answers that are concise and to the point**. Don't issue responses that are too short or too long. Reporters don't want the *War and Peace* version of your message. They need it in bite-size chunks. Deliver it in a message-oriented manner in response to each and every question. At the same time, the press cannot use monosyllabic answers. Number one, it doesn't give them anything to work with. Number two, they may not have time to phrase their next question. Never forget, your replies must be message-driven and succinct.

- **Refuse to address conjecture or "what if" questions**. A media interview is no place for speculation (unless you intend to float a trial balloon of some sort). Don't give the time of day to the theoretical. Stay grounded in the real world. Remain on guard when you hear questions beginning with such phrases as, "Rumor has it ... " or "A source told me ... " The reporter may be fishing, and you do not want to be the one to help them land the big prize. The best way to deflect such subjects is to counter with a phrase of your own, something like, "Let's keep our conversation grounded in the real world ... " or "I'm not much of one for gossip ... " then immediately bridge back to your message. This is important. You are not finished with your answer by simply refusing to be baited. You have a better chance of getting the interview back on your chosen track by reinforcing your message. Remember, our goal is not to guarantee success, but to raise the odds for it. Having the discipline to stick to your message does just that.

- **Never guess at an answer.** This is another example of digging a hole for yourself. I can always tell an interview is about to go sideways when the source says, "I'm not sure, but I would assume ... " You are not there to play guessing games. It goes without saying that you need to keep all the big picture details top of mind. However, you cannot be expected to have every minute fact and figure at your fingertips. It is fine to say you don't know the answer, but never leave it at that. Offer to supply the information later or refer the reporter to the proper source. When you agree to get back to them, do it promptly, otherwise that piece of the puzzle will not make it into the story. Plus, you risk alienating the reporter.

- **Bridge to your message** in response to each challenging question. This technique of "bridging" takes some practice for those who are not accustomed to talking like this in everyday conversations. I've found that my clients grasp it more readily by thinking of it using this construct: Acknowledge → Bridge → Message. Here's how you do that. You must first acknowledge the reporter's question so you cannot be accused of spin. This does not mean you have to agree; far from it. All you are saying is "I hear your question and I respect it." Next, you diplomatically move away from the reporter's question and contention with a transitional bridging phrase (see some examples below). Finally, this paves the road to your message. Immediately follow the bridging phrase with the part of your message that most seamlessly addresses the issue at hand. As you can see, the bridging technique is a smooth way to get things back on the right track.

- **Be prepared with strategic bridging phrases**. What do I mean by a bridging phrase? It's nothing more than a means of transition from the reporter's tough inquiry to the essence of your message. Let's look at an example. You are asked, "Why did your financial results fall so far short of your projections?" You begin by acknowledging: "While it's true the results weren't all we hoped for … " then follow with a bridging phrase: "It is important that we not overlook … " Finally, you are back to your message: "This positions us well for a strong fourth quarter and here's why." We could spend all day coming up with these bridging expressions. Here are some suggestions to get you started: "It's also important to remember," "Let's focus on the big picture," and "I should also remind you." I suggest that you write down a handful of these sayings you are comfortable with, using wording that sounds like you. That way, you'll have them at the ready when you need them.

- **Think of your message as your "safe harbor"** when the questioning gets tough. We all have moments when our brain quits on us for a spell. Maybe you had a bad night's sleep or you're distracted by something back at the office or on the home front. Or maybe you just space out for a few seconds. It happens. What can you do when your mind goes blank in the midst of an interview? Most of the time, you'll find that you retain enough minimal brainpower to recall one of the key components of your message. Go there. That buys you a few seconds to get yourself back on track.

- **Flag your most important ideas** with flagging phrases. You are essentially telling the reporter, "This is what I'm here to talk about" by planting a verbal flag in the ground. Examples include, "The most important thing," "Here's the bottom line," and "If your listeners remember one thing, let it be this." Words like this tend to perk up your listener's ear, whether you are dealing with a reporter or an audience of another sort. It leads them to think something important is about to be imparted. Of course, it is – your message. As with bridging phrases, jot down a list of flagging expressions that reflect your voice. Refuse to let anyone else put their words into your mouth. You need to be genuinely you.

- **Give the reporter a sneak peek** into the area you want to discuss next. The sneak peek entices the reporter to ask a question you want to address. Deliver the sneak peek with a phrase such as, "And that's not all," "I can give you plenty of examples," or, "That's not the end of that story." The reporter may well volley back by asking, "What else is there?" "Give me some examples," or "How does it end?" This is another great technique for gaining control of your interview, keeping it on your chosen track. Will it work every time? Of course not. If it works only half of the time, you are still putting yourself ahead of the game.

- **Deflect questions that are hostile or off-point**. Just because someone asks you a question does not mean you need to answer it. Begin your deflection with a straightforward blocking phrase like "The fact of the matter is," "Let's get to the heart of the issue," or simply, "In fact." Then pivot straight to your message. No trying to wiggle out from under a harsh inquiry. No detours. No ums or ahs. Let me repeat for this is vital when you are confronted with a confrontational question: State your blocking phrase; go right to your message. What happens if the reporter is not satisfied with your response and comes right back at you with essentially the same question? It is your duty to deliver the same answer. They won't like it but, remember, you are not there to make friends. Your job is to consistently broadcast your company's message. Deflecting hostile questions is one way to do that.

- **Stay away from simple "yes" or "no" answers.** Speak in full sentences and state things in your own words while giving the reporter your quotable quote. Even if the reporter proffers the question in words that are music to your ears, you still must feed that back. Keep in mind, the goal here is to get your words and your company's message in the media. It is not often we read a passage similar to this in an article: "When asked if her company's stance would cure cancer, diabetes, and the coronavirus, she replied, 'Yes.'" That's not going to happen. It's not quotable language. Deliver your message and support it with examples in response to every question. As with any rule, there are a couple of exceptions here. If you are trying to wrap up a contentious interview, a curt, monosyllabic answer – or a series of them – sends a signal basically saying, "I'm done with you, buddy." It can also be an effective tactic when you are trying to rattle the reporter by not giving them time to think up their next question. These are rare instances, however.

- **Ask clarifying questions** if you do not understand the reporter's inquiry. Better they tease out any nuances than you try to guess. You may find some using this as a digging technique. Maybe they are trying to determine where the skeletons are buried. Asking a vague question might elicit what they want – and what you want to avoid. On the other hand, it might be a sign of someone inexperienced or unskilled. Perhaps they don't know the right questions to ask. Or (and this is another feature I find particularly annoying) they may not know how to frame a question. They wander. They stop and start. They never get to the point. In that case, feel free to diplomatically hop in and direct the conversation back to your message. Poor reporters may even appreciate your move to get them back on course.

- **Refuse to be rattled by a reporter who interrupts**. I don't know about you, but I hate to be interrupted. Media interview or casual conversation, it really annoys me. As a result, I need to stay alert and not show offense when interruptions take place. Reporters may horn in in the middle of your response for a variety of reasons. They may be pressed for time. They may be signaling that you're not getting to the point. They may be frustrated because you're not giving them what they think they need. Or it may be a conscious technique designed to rattle you. Regardless, wait for the interruption to subside, then complete your response. If disruptions occur throughout your interview, you would be wise to take stock as to why this is happening. And try not to show your annoyance unless the reporter is being blatantly rude. If you believe that to be the case, you can try to stop it in its tracks with a pointed phrase like "As I was saying" or "Let me complete that thought."

- **Remain silent once you have completed your answer**. Don't let the reporter use the silent treatment to bait you into saying something you'll regret seeing in print, online, or on the air. Silence is a tried and true reportorial trap. Most of us are uncomfortable with pregnant pauses. It's how we are wired in our culture. So when a burst of silence takes place, we often rush to fill it. Avoid the temptation during media interviews. If you are satisfied with your answer, stand firm, smile, and wait for the next question. Leave it to the reporter to fill the gap. You encounter a few seconds of quiet? Big deal. The only thing you will do by bumbling and stumbling through a clumsy addendum is to dig yourself a great big hole. Let your message-driven reply stand. An ancillary part of this trick is for the reporter to continue jotting down notes, seemingly busy while in reality waiting to see if you will break the silence. Don't. I will admit that this was one of my favorite techniques during my days as a reporter. Why? It works. I still use it frequently when conducting simulated interviews as part of a messaging or media skills workshop.

Post-interview Pursuits

- **Debrief your performance immediately** after each interview. This pertains to both real-world reporter interviews and those you conduct during informal practice sessions. Feedback will never be as fresh. Take a cold-eyed look at the key elements: How successful were you at imparting your message? How effective were your nonverbal tools? What worked for you? What can stand an upgrade? Solicit feedback far and wide. You never know who will come up with a previously unmined gem. Ask for candor and emphasize that you are interested in improving, regardless of how you performed.

- **Realize that not all feedback is created equal.** You will hear things not worth heeding. You need to run it through your own filter to ascertain its value. Two people who must absolutely be a part of this assessment process are your chief communications officer and your communications strategy and training consultant. These experts have the depth of knowledge (or at least they should) capable of offering solid counsel.

- **Record all media interviews as they take place.** Nothing fancy needed; a small recorder or your mobile device will do the job. The laws for recording telephone interviews vary from state to state, so familiarize yourself with your jurisdiction's edicts. Note well that this also applies to video interviews over services like Skype and Zoom. Many reporters routinely record their exchanges. You have the same right. This serves a couple of purposes. First, it leaves you with a record of the exchange. Should any disputed quotes arise, you'll have proof of exactly what was said. In addition, it can be a great means of advancing your sustained professional development. Listen back to the recording immediately afterward and assess the positives and negatives. Go back to it every now and then and compare it with later interviews to gauge how you are progressing as a media source. As always, shine a light on those positives in future interviews, and work to improve the shortfalls over the long run.

- **Arrange for a colleague or family member** to capture your radio or TV broadcast. That provides you with a copy for your archives. Most televised interviews will be available online. Rare is the TV station or network that does not do so. Still, it is a good idea to make your own recording just in case. If you are unable to record it yourself, ask the producer or reporter when they expect to air it and post it on their website. They may not know yet, but it can't hurt to ask. These archives are among the best professional development tools you have.

- **Don't pester a journalist** by asking when your piece will appear in print or on the air. As noted above, sometimes they just don't know. Or, if they think they do, they may find the story bumped for more urgent news. Editors, not individual reporters, control the news flow. It is fine to ask once at the conclusion of your interview, but don't inundate them with daily calls or emails checking on the status. You will be labeled a pest and the odds of them contacting you for comment in the future will dwindle.

- **Contact the reporter directly** if you feel a clarification, correction, or retraction is necessary. If they made a mistake, you owe them the chance to rectify matters. You will find the difference among those three levels in Chapter Six's Reporter's Glossary.

- **Approach the editor** for a correction only if you gain no satisfaction from the reporter. And give the latter the courtesy of telling them that you plan to get in touch with their boss. There are two reasons for this. First, it is common civility. Second, it can smooth your future relationship with the newsperson. You may need them – and they may need you – down the road, so don't burn that bridge. If you fail to get your desired response from the editor, pat yourself on the back for fighting the good fight, and acknowledge the fact that they are the ones who hold the controls. Make your best case. Don't make any needless enemies. Move on to your next campaign.

Creating a First-class Media Relations Operation

- **Bring your communications staffer** with you to an interview whenever possible. They can take care of any logistics, such as getting you to the right place, recording the proceedings, and stepping in to redirect things if need be. This leaves you free to concentrate on driving home your message. What if your interview is over the phone? Include that staffer on the line, and have the good manners to let the reporter know they are listening in. They can tactfully prompt you if you forget to note a key point and can send the reporter any necessary follow up material. In addition, your communications shop works hard to establish relationships with reporters. Including them in the process helps here. This redounds to your company's benefit.

- **Showcase your expertise and on-camera talents** by cataloging recordings of your previous interviews. Start with some local TV appearances or lower risk interviews. Share the clips with your communications staff so they can begin to pitch you to higher profile media outlets when appropriate.

- **Know when to pull back and stick with a written statement.** Assenting to interviews is not always the right call. If you get the sense you are about to be caught in a trap or that you risk opening a can of worms albeit unintentionally, the smart call may be to forgo the face-to-face in favor of a statement. Also, if you believe a provocative issue might lack "legs" – an ability to sustain itself over an extended period – and could blow over quickly and quietly, why fan the flames? Distributing a message-oriented statement demonstrates responsiveness while keeping the temperature low.

- **Use embargoes sparingly**. This is a technique whereby you turn on the faucet to let your news flow while not wanting it to become public until later. This is best used for complex issues that will take reporters some time to digest or when you want to give them time to do some additional digging. Be aware that, just because you label something as embargoed, news outlets do not have to abide by your wishes unless they have expressly agreed to that condition ahead of time.

- **Be judicious about giving certain reporters exclusives**. Journalists tend, as a group, to be thin-skinned. They are also competitive. Granting an exclusive to one means shutting out everyone else, whether dangling a jump on a high-profile story or an interview with a prominent personality. That larger cohort of reporters may not appreciate you giving their rivals an advantage. When might you grant an exclusive? If you are likely to get front page coverage in *The Wall Street Journal* or the lead story on one of the network nightly news broadcasts, go for it. Just go into it with your eyes open to the fact that you may alienate some scribes you might need down the road.

- **Hold firm to any ground rules** you agreed to in advance, such as whether they can take a tour of your office or plant. Appoint an escort (or, if the train starts to go off the rails, an enforcer), someone not afraid to stand up to a challenge. Ideally, this is one of your senior media relations staff. If the reporter tries to stray into forbidden territory or talk with someone not licensed to be one of your spokespeople, remind them of the agreed-upon ground rules, and steer them politely but firmly back on course. You had an agreement. Don't consent to any unilateral – and potentially dangerous – spur-of-the-moment deviations.

- **Update your media strategy** to take into account recent developments like the minute-by-minute news cycle in which news is posted immediately on the web and digital media. The label of the "24-hour news cycle" came into vogue some time ago. It fit when CNN was still a novelty. For some time now, I've preferred to use the term "Minute-by minute News Cycle" as it is more reflective of our times. We no longer rely on gathering around the network TV evening news broadcasts or the morning newspaper landing on the front porch. Media outlets now cannibalize their own products with incessant updates on their websites and on their digital media channels. Smart media sources are sensitive to these changes and structure their media relations operations to align with them.

- **Decide whether you can or want to bypass the traditional press.** As digital media tools proliferate and gain acceptance, some businesses now communicate with no filter, bypassing the traditional media altogether. Your company, in essence, creates its own media network, developing content and pushing it through numerous digital pipelines. The creator decides which campaigns to launch, which to cancel, and which to expand. It is somewhat akin to a television network touting its new fall lineup or axing underperforming shows.

- **Fine tune your digital presence**, but never remove it from your overall communications strategy. Digital media channels are just tools and tactics – nothing more, nothing less. Do not buy into the canard that you need solely young people to execute digitally. Success comes only when you craft a strategy first, then deploy the relevant tactics and tools. Should you tap the insights of younger staffers? In some cases, sure. And they may well be more proficient at using some of the tools. But – and this is really important – they are unlikely to have developed the strategic insights your overall media plan demands. Listen? Yes. Develop their talents over time? Sure. Entrust the success of your business and public policy goals exclusively to untested hands? Not a chance.

- **Decide in advance which bloggers**, if any, you will treat as accredited journalists at your meetings, at news conferences, and for interview purposes. In my view, few bloggers should qualify. I publish the C-suite Blueprint blog, but that doesn't make me a journalist (despite the fact that I was one once upon a time). It's up to the blogger to convince you that they belong in the media category. Just because they request credentials doesn't mean you have to issue them. Ask if they have been certified by other reputable organizations. Perhaps they have a press pass from one of the Congressional press galleries, your state legislature, or the state police. Conduct some due diligence. And be aware that there are some shady outfits that ostensibly certify legitimacy. These are just press pass mills that endorse anyone who pays a fee. Check to ensure that any credentials submitted to you have the imprimatur of a valid authority.

- **Stay "on the record"** unless you are a front-line communications pro accustomed to negotiating ground rules with journalists. This means everything you say and do is fair game for inclusion in the story. What does on the record mean? My research report, *Can We Talk Off the Record? Resolving Disagreements, Increasing Understanding Between Reporters and Public Relations Practitioners,* puts forth this definition: "Anything a source says can be quoted and any information supplied can be used with no restrictions. Documents and nonverbal signals are also fair game. Unless there is a compelling reason forbidding it, on the record interviews are the safest way to proceed." To reinforce: This is the default for every single media exchange. Whenever you are in the presence of a reporter – whether during an arranged interview or a casual encounter at a cocktail soirée – you are subject to being quoted.

- **(Note: This tip applies to front-line media relations staff only) Agree upon any ground rules and get a positive assent** from the reporter. Define in advance what terms of art like, "on background," "off-the-record," or "not for attribution" mean to both of you. You will find consensus definitions for each in the Reporter's Glossary in Chapter Six.

- **Guard your hiring process.** While discussing the subject of personnel, it is a good idea to build into your hiring process the need for including past reporters among your communications staff. Charge the senior communications experts with the screening and hiring. On a related note, they should also be the ones to contract with your media strategy consultants; this in consultation with your C-suite since they need to have a comfort level, too. Never cede this responsibility to another department.

Engaging Your Media Strategy Consultant

- **Insist upon media training** for all executives and public-facing workers. You are better positioned to achieve your organizational and career goals when taking to heart effective messaging and communications skills. Just be sure you don't stop with a lone workshop. Too many companies make this mistake, thinking that their top executives have been "media trained" (that catchphrase really rubs me the wrong way) after participating in a single session. Smart companies realize that message review and communications skill development – or any professional development opportunity, for that matter – can be successful only when it is a sustained endeavor. Sure, most people will likely be somewhat improved following one workshop. The fact is lasting improvement comes with time and dedication. Don't let your company fall victim to the one-off tragedy. Any reputable consultant should emphasize this. If they don't, they are either ignorant or they don't care about your success with the press. Look elsewhere.

- **Determine whether your media strategy and training consultant customizes each program** exclusively for you or offers only cookie cutter approaches. You have only one guess as to which approach best benefits your business. Some examples: I customize every session. Sure, there are common elements – message development and delivery, simulated interviews, and the beginnings of that vital sustained professional development plan. Yet the emphasis on each of these elements can vary dramatically depending on the company and its needs. It is important to highlight that the mix for each workshop depends on the participants' experience, abilities, and attitudes. Years ago, I worked as a media training subcontractor for a global public relations agency. They offered the same agenda for every client. I felt straightjacketed (and no longer work with them). Furthermore, it bothered me that the client was not getting the best they could get.

- **Ask lots of questions of your prospective media strategy and training consultant**. For instance: Are you dedicated to training, or do you spread yourself thin doing lots of other things, too? What books and articles have you written that demonstrate your thought leadership? Over the years, I've witnessed "PR" generalists try to persuade prospective clients that they are capable of leading a strategic media training program. Guess again. They may be perfectly capable of pitching reporters or writing news releases. But taking the lead on such a critical professional development initiative? No, thank you. The best consultants are committed – and will ask you to commit – to a sustained professional development regimen. This can involve anything from multiple formal workshops over time to periodic check-ins. I offer a host of essential questions in "A Buyer's Guide to Media Strategy Consultants."

- **Take advantage of regular checkups** to ensure your skills remain sharp and you don't pick up any bad habits. As noted earlier, there is no such thing as being "media trained." Enhancing your interview skills is a lifelong endeavor that takes commitment. True pros follow a path to lifelong learning. This is not to say that you need to partake of a formal workshop every quarter (though in some cases – particularly with executives newly promoted to high profile positions – that may be advised). It can consist of occasional telephone or video checkups, practice rounds with internal staff, or reading recommendations. The point is sustained improvement comes only with sustained attention. Yes, I sound like a broken record. It's critical. Make sure the consultants you choose understand this and are steadfast in their commitment to it.

CHAPTER 6

A Reporter's Glossary

Every profession has its own jargon and terms of art. Reporters are no different. Everyone from the C-suite to the most junior news source needs to understand the lingo.

Former reporters should have an edge here. Indeed, if your communications shop lacks the presence of an ex-reporter, you are operating at a distinct disadvantage.

In the interest of consistency, you would be wise to adopt these definitions for key journalistic words and phrases.

I encourage you to use this glossary when engaging in your business deals with the press. You'll not only be able to cut through some of the clutter, you'll also appear more informed and, in the reporter's eyes, more capable.

Above the fold: Literally, this refers to a newspaper article that appears on the top half of the front page. Figuratively, it connotes a big news story.

Actuality: Radio sound bites that generally last only a few seconds, though they can run longer when warranted.

Anchor: The star who delivers the day's news on television or radio, and is responsible – along with producers – for maintaining the flow of the newscast. They often put questions to guests on the air, so should be skilled interviewers.

Assignment editor: This behind-the-scenes individual is the heart of the newsroom. They decide which reporters, videographers, and photographers cover which stories.

B-roll: Background footage used for cutaways in a video package. If a camera crew comes to you, they may ask you to do things like work at your desk or walk along a hallway or sidewalk while trying to look natural. They need this footage for cutaways during the editing purposes.

Beat: The topic covered by a particular reporter. For instance, they may be assigned the Capitol Hill beat, the environmental beat, or the business beat.

Bumper: A short snippet of video used in TV newscasts that leads into and out of commercial breaks. It's sometimes used as a teaser to keep viewers tuned in.

Byline: Simply put, it's the name of the journalist who reported the story.

Clarification: This occurs when a media outlet needs to clear up confusion in one of its reports, even if the facts are technically correct. It's an acknowledgment that they missed a detail or mischaracterized something, and allows them to better explain the original story or add new perspective. Note that most publications have corrections policies that place them prominently in print and online, but not all apply the same process to clarifications.

Clip: A news story that you have – literally or figuratively – cut from a publication for distribution to your C-suite executives. Clips also come in audio, video, and web form.

Copy: The verbiage turned in by reporters. Editors have been known to scream – either verbally or electronically – "Get me that copy, now!"

Correction: An admission that "We blew it." You have the right to ask for a clarification or correction if you believe you've been wronged. Be aware that some media outlets don't like to admit their mistakes, so be prepared with the evidence when you ask.

Cutline: Often called a caption, this text below a photo describes the action.

Dateline: This indicates the city and, in many cases, the state or country where the story originates.

Daybook: One of a reporter's most precious tools, wire services like the Associated Press and Reuters issue daily daybooks that tell where and when newsy events take place.

Deadline: The absolute drop dead moment the reporter needs your input. If you miss a deadline, you are out of the story. Plus, you've made that reporter question your value for future articles.

Editor: The boss of a newsroom. Reporters have been known to tremble at the mere mention of their editor's name.

Editorial: A column advocating a newspaper's position on important matters of the day. In most major news operations, there is an inviolable firewall between the editorial board and the newsroom. Reporters do not know the contents of the day's editorials before they are published.

Embargo: When you and the reporter specifically agree to hold a story for publication until a date and time certain. You should use this technique only with scribes you trust implicitly.

Exclusive: When you agree to give one reporter a story before the rest of the pack. Use caution here for you can easily alienate journalists by giving an exclusive to a competitor.

Feature: A human interest story that usually lacks significant hard news value.

First Amendment: The part of the U.S. constitution that assures a free press. It reads, in toto, "Congress shall make no law respecting an establishment of religion, or prohibiting the free exercise thereof; or abridging the freedom of speech, or of the press; or the right of the people peaceably to assemble, and to petition the Government for a redress of grievances."

Freelancer: A reporter who works for a variety of publications, not employed solely by one. Freelancers may be highly knowledgeable about your issues or may know nothing whatsoever, so look into their portfolio before you engage with them.

Front-page news: The biggest stories with the boldest headlines go here. This term is used both literally and figuratively.

Green room: Backstage at a TV studio, you'll find a room for upcoming guests to cool their heels and, more importantly, to prepare for their appearance. When you visit the green room, avoid the food spread; you're there to be part of a news story, not to nosh (besides, who needs poppy seeds from that bagel between your teeth when you appear on camera?).

Grip and grin: This staged photo is the classic handshake shot, often used by politicians and celebrities when they deign to interact with riff raff like you and me. I typically eschew these shots in favor of more real-world poses.

Headline (also called header): This appears at the top of an article or news release. It is essential for attracting a reader and should, in as few words as possible, highlight the main point of your message.

Head shot: A formal photo that shows you in business attire from the shoulders up. All executives should have an up to date head shot taken by a professional photographer at the ready. Avoid casual poses or pictures of you with your kids or dogs. You are aiming for a professional image, not that of a best buddy.

IFB: The earpiece you wear when participating in a satellite media tour or TV network guest appearance when multiple guests are piped in from several locations. It stands for interruptible foldback. This is the same device you see in the ears of TV anchors and of reporters in the field.

Journalist: A person who reports for any media outlet – print, broadcast, or online. Reporters, editors, photographers, and videographers all fall into this classification.

Jump: When a newspaper leads with a story on page one then continues it inside, that continuation is the jump page. It's a longstanding clever means of putting more content on the front page.

Kicker: Typically a light story that ends a radio or television news broadcast. It often features either a feel-good human interest dimension or a quirky angle.

Lede: The first sentence or idea of a news article. And no, it's not a misspelling. The word originated in the 19th century when newspapers used hot lead type. The typesetters would get confused whether their editors meant the hot "lead" type or the "lead" of the article. Some clever soul decided to change the spelling of the article's beginning. Now you can regale friends with this bit of trivia at your next soirée.

Letter to the editor: Itching to get something off your chest? Write a letter to the editor. Your odds are pretty good in smaller publications. If you're aiming for the likes of *The New York Times*, however, you will need luck on your side.

Media relations: The practice of dealing with the press, ideally carried out by former reporters turned communications experts who know how reporters think and what they need. Sadly, not all organizations employ such experienced hands.

Media training: A series of strategic professional development workshops that show executives how to deal with the press. It should, at a minimum, cover messaging and communications skills enhancement, and offer simulated practice interviews. Conscientious consultants also include a long-term program capable of sustaining improvement over time.

News advisory: When you need to notify the press of a forthcoming newsworthy event, you issue a news advisory that includes its date, time, and place.

News conference: Also called a press conference, businesses hold these when they want to announce news to all reporters at the same time in the same place.

News director: They run radio and TV newsrooms. Assignment editors, editors, camera crews, producers, and reporters all answer to them. Title creep being what it is, some local TV news departments now have vice presidents of news; same thing.

News hole: Print publications only have so many pages. TV and radio news broadcasts only have so much time. That's called the news hole, and it is shrinking in nearly all forms of traditional media.

News release (also called press release): A brief written document issued to the press announcing your latest news. Keep these brief regardless of how much regulatory verbiage you have to regurgitate; long news releases tend to go straight into most reporters' circular files.

Not for attribution: The reporter may publish information provided by sources. The source can be quoted, though not by name. The reporter and communications expert must negotiate how the source will be identified (e.g., a company vice president, a source familiar with the negotiations).

Off the record: Nothing provided off the record can be used in print or broadcast. This is most frequently used to steer reporters in a particular direction while attempting to leave no fingerprints. Only experienced communicators should go off the record, and then only if they know and trust the reporter and media outlet.

On background: The reporter can use freely any information a source provides, either orally or in writing. However, the reporter cannot quote the source either by name or by other identification. Going on background is useful for individuals on the front lines of media relations who prefer that quotes come from others in the company.

On the record: Anything a source says can be quoted and any information supplied can be used with no restrictions. Note well that this is the default option for all media exchanges. Documents, wall hangings, overheard conversations, and nonverbal signals – such as a grimace or chuckle – are also fair game. Unless there is a compelling reason arguing against it, on the record interviews are the safest way to proceed.

Op-ed: Literally, opposite the editorial page. This is where guest writers can air their grievances and where the newspaper's regular columnists are found. Guest slots go most frequently to those with name recognition or with large organizations that lend them some legitimacy.

Package: The entirety of a video news piece, as in, "Let's run that package on the 11:00 broadcast."

Pitch: When you try to get a reporter interested in your story, you are making a pitch.

Podcast: Prepare for these downloadable interview programs much as you would a radio talk show appearance.

Press conference (*see news conference*)

Press kit: The assemblage of materials designed to give reporters pertinent information about your business generally or about your specific issues. It can include news releases, fact sheets, executive bios, B-roll video, and a host of other items.

Press release (*see news release*)

Producer: The individual who actually makes decisions about and puts together a broadcast news piece. While the reporter gets all the face time, the producer does much of the heavy lifting. You would be wise to establish solid relationships with producers.

Pronouncer: A phonetic spelling intended to help broadcast reporters avoid embarrassing blunders (e.g., former Speaker of the House John Boehner (bay' ner)). Use these in your news releases when warranted.

Public affairs: This encompasses such fields as government relations, public policy, and lobbying.

Public relations: An attempt to influence the public with non-paid tactics, though that line has been blurred in recent years.

Pull quote: Where a publication highlights a particularly juicy quotation by putting it in a box alongside the body of the article.

Radio media tour (RMT): This takes place when you talk remotely with a bunch of radio stations, one after the other. RMTs can be done either by telephone or in a broadcast studio.

Retraction: When a media outlet really blows it, they'll issue a retraction, in effect saying the story should never have been printed or broadcast.

Satellite media tour (SMT): You sit in a studio that is often the size of a broom closet and are interviewed remotely by TV stations from across the country. You'll stare into a camera while listening to your interviewer through an earpiece (known as an IFB; see above).

Scoop: Reporters live for scoops. Being the first to get a big story puts them and their outlet in a bright, shiny light.

Scrum: Occurs when a pack of reporters swarms a source, usually jostling and shouting questions with cameras whirring.

Sidebar: An adjunct to the main article, usually placed in a box next to the main story.

Sound bite: The juiciest of juicy quotes on audio or video. Sound bite lengths have been shrinking in recent decades, so ensure yours are tight and concise.

Source: That's you, the individual a reporter turns to in an effort to gain information.

Spin: Trying to pull the wool over a reporter's eyes by spinning them rarely works. Spin is a sin, so avoid it at all costs.

Standup: A television reporter delivering news on air from the field. It can be a live feed or a segment of a package.

Stringer: Most often a part-time or freelance reporter in a city removed from the home base. For instance, a local newspaper might employ a stringer to follow its Congressional delegation in Washington, D.C.

TelePrompTer: Although TV news anchors look like they are staring directly at you when reading the news, they are in reality reading from a TelePrompTer located just above, below, or alongside the camera. It offers the illusion of eye contact while staying on script. TelePrompTers can also be used when speaking in public in large halls.

Video news release (VNR): You already know what a news release is. A VNR is done in video form.

Wire service: These services deliver news to media outlets. They offer local, national, and international feeds, and include such other features as sports, weather, and lifestyle. The leading wire services in the U.S. are the Associated Press (AP) and Reuters.

CHAPTER 7

Mending Your Media Health

Chapter Four covered the basic interview formats you are liable to encounter. Now let us turn to helping you prepare for these specific types of business deals with journalists.

Following are some of my favorite exercises designed to help you sharpen your media relations edge. Return to this section often and use the drill that befits your current situation. Don't be afraid to mix it up. Practice one format today. Try another next week. Turn to a different one next month. This approach helps to give broad exposure to the various setups while keeping your professional development attitude fresh.

Taking Inventory

We all hold various strengths and weaknesses when it comes to communicating in public. The key to improving your abilities lies in maximizing strengths and minimizing vulnerabilities.

This exercise can help to heighten your nonverbal performance by using your Video Tools and Audio Tools. This handy checklist is designed to remind you which are strengths that you need to maintain, and which are challenges you may wish to sharpen.

You have two choices with the tools that you place on your sharpen list: 1) Work to transform them from liabilities to assets or 2) minimize their use in favor of other tools.

Place an "M" next to those tools you need to maintain. Mark an "S" next to those you want to sharpen. Commit to working on your "S" list over the long run.

Video Tools

- Action
- Facial expression
- Eye contact
- Wardrobe
- Props

Audio Tools

- Pitch
- Articulation
- Volume
- Emotion
- Rate

Note: Refuse to overload yourself. That will only result in frustration. Be mindful of addressing only one challenge at a time. As that tool becomes sharper, move on to the next one on your list. Take this quiz again in a few months and compare the results with today's. You are likely to see that you have sharpened a few skills.

News Conference

During this exercise, you assume the role of one being questioned at a news conference. Make sure the setting is lifelike – get a lectern with a microphone and set up some chairs for the reporters. It also helps to bring in some cameras and bright lights.

Then assemble as many office mates as you can and arm them with tough questions about your issues. Insist that they fire those salvos at you to gauge not only how you reply to questions, but also how you control the crowd of hungry journalists, and how you bring the news conference to a graceful close.

Radio Talk Show or Podcast

Set up your conference room as a mock radio studio. You do not need a large conference facility for this one; most real-life studios are very cozy.

Next, break out some microphones and set them on the table. You are the guest. A colleague portrays the host. Make sure your host sticks to the agreed upon time limits. Radio is highly inflexible when it comes to end times. Ten minutes means exactly that; not nine minutes and 55 seconds or 10 minutes and two seconds.

You can pretend your program is five minutes long or a full hour. Hint: The shorter the format, the more challenging it is to fit your messages into the allotted time.

For an added twist, have some additional co-workers call in with listener questions. Script them in advance and make sure some are at least mildly challenging.

An audio recording of this is sufficient for purposes of assessing feedback since your Audio Tools are key when serving as a radio guest.

Field Interview

If you anticipate that television reporters may visit you on location, make sure to take advantage of this exercise. Assign one individual to act as the reporter and another to serve as the videographer. Your reporter should use a hand-held microphone to conduct a stand-up interview for five to 10 minutes.

This will give you a sense of how comfortable you are with this format and what aspects of your performance need attention. Additionally, it should give you a better idea of what it takes to talk in concise quotable quotes.

Ask some routine questions as well as some tough ones in order to gauge responses to various issues. Also, instruct your reporter to crowd you (although in an era of social distancing this is not feasible). This will give you a feel for the small amount of personal space offered in many interview situations.

As with all of these exercises, be sure to view the video immediately upon completion of the interview. For extra insight, watch a brief section with the sound turned off, asking, "If I saw this person on TV, would I watch the interview or would I hit the remote button and zap it?"

Satellite Media Tour

Use a tiny conference room for this SMT exercise. Why? Some of the real-life studios you will encounter are the size of broom closets (then again, some are held in spacious studios). Place your camera on a tripod and lock it down.

Go through a number of fast-paced interviews in rapid succession. Reference something about the city you are speaking to – a figure relevant to that geographical area or a locally-based anecdote or third-party reference.

Assign someone to write out which city the interview is being beamed to along with the name of both the interviewer and the station. Place it in full view.

I'll give you bonus points if someone finds an IFB to place in your ear (and even more points if you work with a video crew with the ability to pipe audio into the IFB). You don't have an IFB lying around? Use another wired ear bud, but insert it in only one ear, clipping the wire to the back collar as would happen in real time.

Video Conference Interview

Skype and Zoom interviews are ever more common these days. Treat your preparations for these much as you would for an SMT.

The major wrinkle? Rehearse with your computer or mobile device. Since every device has its quirks, use the very same one you plan to use for the real thing.

Most of the time you will not have the advantage of being in a studio, so you must provide for your own camera, microphone, and backdrop. Aim for as professional a quality as you can without going overboard. A basic HD camera and a good standalone microphone should do the trick.

One important note: Locate your camera's lens and hold steady and persistent eye contact with it. Do not look at your screen or monitor as that often throws off the direction of your gaze.

Editorial Board Visit

One often ignored media outreach tool is the process of sitting down with your editorial board, the people who write your local newspaper's editorials, to brief them on your point of view.

Most of these visits are freewheeling discussions that take place around a conference table. Editors (and sometimes reporters) toss out questions, seemingly at random sometimes. You should aim, in this exercise, for the same type of atmosphere.

Your job here is to convey your main messages surrounding a hot issue facing your company. The assignment is to convince the editors to write a favorable editorial on this issue.

Who plays the editors? Seek out colleagues who know how to guide a discussion. In this case, they should try to turn the discussion to other subjects. This is bound to happen in the real world, and you need to assess the ability to pull the dialogue back on topic.

Record this interview to video, but do not let the camera be a focus. And, as always, play back and critique the video immediately, looking first to enhance strengths, then to address challenges.

Actualities

This exercise is intended to sharply focus attention on talking in concise, message-oriented sound bites when interviewed by a radio reporter over the telephone. Your reporter in this scenario zeroes in on a single topic currently in the headlines, given that radio reporters deal almost exclusively with breaking news.

The interview should be exceptionally brief, lasting two to three minutes. Such a short interview forces you to get your message across quickly and efficiently. If you don't, it will be evident when the recording is reviewed.

An audio recording is fine when it comes time for assessing feedback here. The important thing is to weigh the delivery of your message and the quality of your Audio Tools.

The Ambush

Here's one your media relations staff should organize if you are expecting tough sledding with the media.

Assign one person to portray a television reporter and another to serve as the camera operator. Catch your spokesperson unaware and ambush them with your camera rolling and microphone in their face. Surprise them as they step off an elevator, enter your building, or get out of their car in the parking lot.

Toss all the prickly questions you can. See how they think on their feet, noting in particular how much of the message they impart and how they use Video Tools and Audio Tools.

Important note: You must gauge whether your executives will accept this type of exercise. Some don't like surprises, especially ones that may not show them in the most favorable light. In stark terms, you don't want people losing their jobs over this.

The Third Degree

When the going gets tough and you are facing a crisis situation, the only way to prepare is to relentlessly subject yourself to the most negative, hostile questions you can muster.

Sit behind a table or stand in the front of a room (preferably with

TV lights blazing) and try to fend off barbed inquiries. Make this a no-holds-barred session. It's better to get accustomed to the hardballs in the security of a training environment than to be caught oblivious in the real world.

Pay particular attention to keeping your cool. Remember, this is a business deal that demands a professional demeanor. Note your success at consistently returning to message, and the skill of serving as traffic cop when dealing with the barrage of questioners.

When you are preparing for crisis mode, I highly recommend you run this drill a number of times.

Walk a Mile in My Shoes

My clients always have fun with this one. It allows them to experience firsthand reporters' deadlines, the need for fact checking, and the attitude of some sources toward the press.

In this role reversal exercise, you and a colleague act as reporters, taking turns interviewing each other. In Round One, Spokesperson A plays reporter, interviewing Spokesperson B. For Round Two, switch roles.

Get a third person to act as the editor. Make sure your editor is a real stickler for snappy ledes and airtight facts – everything a real editor would demand. As an honorary newshound, you will be under extremely tight deadline pressure.

Here is the assignment:
- Ten minutes to review materials and develop questions.
- Five minutes to interview one another.
- Ten minutes to write the headline, lede, and most quotable quote from the interview.

Articles are submitted to the editor, who orders appropriate corrections. If your editor is not satisfied with the outcome, you can give each reporter another five minutes to follow up with their interviewee. They will soon get a notion of what it is like to walk a mile in the reporter's shoes.

CHAPTER 8

Emerging from the Pandemic

Picture this scenario a few days, weeks, or months down the road. You've managed to struggle back to the office after a coronavirus-imposed work period from home. You just can't quite get into the flow. Neither can your office mates.

Oh, the water cooler chatter helps (even though you are standing six feet apart) as does the simple joy of connecting with others face to face (or at least mask to mask). Still, the fact remains you need to keep your distance. No welcoming handshakes or sharing of a communal box of doughnuts.

Smart businesses are getting in shape for the day – whenever it arrives – that the news cycle shifts, when the front pages and lead stories turn back to things other than the pandemic, economic collapse, and social justice issues. In other words, they are preparing to take advantage of the news ecology. At some point, newsrooms are going to be eager for your stories again.

The important point to all of this: Structure a routine capable of keeping your skills in tune now, and preparing for a successful emergence as the pandemic-related restrictions ease.

Preparing for the Day

Your communications skills – other than those now-tedious Zoom calls – have not been honed appropriately in months. It's time to get them back to work once again so you are ready when those headlines shift. Whether you are in the habit of interacting with reporters, delivering presentations, or advocating before policymakers, your communications abilities need regular maintenance. And you have not been able to get them into the shop lately.

You may not have needed to fill up your gas tank or check the pressure in your tires in a while. That means that auto repair shops will be busy with deferred maintenance. You've got to do it to get your car in good running order.

Just remember to treat yourself – in this case, your professional self – better than you treat your possessions. Tend to your rusty communications skills with the same tender, loving care you give Fluffy, who is already scheduled for her annual checkup with the vet.

You owe it to yourself and your company. To get back in the swing of things, take advantage of a rigorous media strategy, presentation skills, or advocacy checkup. Otherwise, you will be hard pressed to perform at a high level when dealing with the press or fighting for your public policy goals.

Where Are You Now?

Curious where you stand after this pandemic-necessitated lapse? Try this simple test: Record on your mobile device a rehearsal for the next presentation you plan to deliver. I would wager that you will hear the same annoying catch phrase creeping in time and again. Or some long pauses that were not there previously when you were in top form. Or that omnipresent "y'know" that you worked so hard to get rid of has sneaked back into your lexicon.

But you're still fine when talking to the press, you say? Okay, try this: Take a quick scan of articles or video clips in which you were quoted in pre-coronavirus days. Are your quotes as sharp now? Are your words as vivid? Are your stories to the point? Without some practice to round into shape, your quotes may no longer make the cut.

There is no shame in acknowledging that your communications tools have a layer of dust on them. We are all in the same boat. Smart communicators know that those talents demand regular sharpening, and now is the time to get moving. You may need a sit-down with your chief communications officer, a media skills refresher, or a months-long graduate level presentation skills curriculum. Whatever your skill level, you will see improvement only if you buckle down and work for it – starting right now.

Step Inside the Real World

Need more persuasion that a continuing education plan is in order? Allow me to share a positive real-life example about a pro who embraces a program of sustained professional development. I have taught one physician, a thought leader in his field of cancer research, multiple times. Whenever we get together, he takes notes, asks questions, and is always in learning mode. The result? He nails his quotes nearly every time he talks to reporters.

Now let me tell the regrettable tale of an executive who, while well respected, had neglected to refresh his media skills on a regular basis. During his first brush up in six years (!), it became clear that cobwebs covered even the most basic of his skills. In addition, he had a good deal of difficulty broadcasting his message, both in his workshop and in the real world. Don't let this be you.

One more example. I always request pre-training feedback before beginning work with a new client. This gives me a better sense of how experienced the participants are and what goals they are aiming for. I am surprised by how often those who tell me they have taken part in a previous workshop evidence a low skill level. Some have only a hazy memory of attending one lone session previously, unable to recall exactly when it was or who led the proceedings. Not surprisingly, there is often a correlation between their memory of the last formal instruction and the rustiness of their talents.

Staying in Shape

The coronavirus contagion has thrown a wrench into many a company's communications and public affairs plans. Any stab at long-term – or even short-term – planning is liable to result only in wasted effort.

What might it take to emerge from our pandemic in reasonably solid business shape? Here's what I'm recommending to clients (and anyone else who will listen). Focus on these two things:

1. Commit to keeping your communications skills sharp. This applies to your C-suite leadership, media relations staff, and roster of issue experts who deal with the press. What can you do to stay fresh?

    - Review videos of your past media interviews and presentations to assess what's working and what's not.

    - Schedule regular video calls between your media relations staff and spokespeople to update your messaging, hash out budding issues, and exercise that Q&A muscle.

    - Are you homebound with a bright college or high school student? Enlist them to engage you in Q&A (the young tend to be more skeptical, so this should keep you on your toes).

    - Sharpen your video conferencing skills so that, when a remote media interview opportunity pops up, you are ready.

2. Position your company to emerge from the crisis as whole as possible.

    - Sketch out what you want your message to sound like when you hatch from your cocoon.

    - Recognize that you'll need to adjust matters when the time comes.

    - Gain the edge. Make this a priority now. Your competitors may not be doing likewise.

Stay Sharp. Get Ready.

It has become clear to me lately that trying to plan for anything beyond tomorrow (and I mean that literally) is an exercise in futility. The plain fact is we have no idea what the future holds, let alone what our business world will look like months or years down the road.

As I noted earlier, I had to rearrange my book publication plans. Talk about a major business decision. I never dreamed of having to make that move even 10 days prior.

The communications skills of C-suite and other spokespeople will erode with the passage of time and lack of normal practice activity. Let's face it. A chief communications officer or top government relations hand can no longer drop by the C-suite to bounce around an idea or offer a snap Q&A session.

Necessity is the mother of invention, the old saying goes. With face-to-face meetings and training workshops temporarily waylaid, you've got to make the best of what you've got.

Whether dealing with the media, delivering presentations (particularly with so many executives unschooled in how to present on video conferencing tools like Skype, Webex, and Zoom), or keeping advocacy efforts fine tuned, companies need to dig deep for creative ways of staying on point.

In addition, your messages are likely to be shifting faster than ever. How can you keep pace with what you need to communicate to customers, the press, policymakers, and other stakeholders? Below are examples of issues to tackle – ideas that will keep your skills as sharp as possible in the moment:

- How to adapt your communications and public affairs strategies during this extended crisis
- What you can do to prepare for the new business world once the crisis abates
- Messaging techniques that help preserve your business and public policy goals

- The proper way to act when participating in a video conference
- Best practices for organizing and leading video conference discussions
- Methods for keeping communications skills sharp when times are tough
- How to keep your communications team intact as they work from home
- A review of your company's current communications strengths and challenges
- A review of your personal communications strengths and challenges
- How to forge a sustained professional development program that takes you through the current crisis and beyond
- Digging into resources – books, blogs, articles, videos, and podcasts – that stimulate your learning
- Public policy steps you can realistically take – and not take – working remotely
- How to shine a light on your communications strengths
- Long-term strategies for dealing with communications shortfalls
- What reporters need to hear – and not hear – from you
- Effective response management techniques for dealing with Q&A
- How to prepare for media interviews conducted by telephone or video
- For communications professionals only: How to safely negotiate off the record, on background, and not for attribution interviews
- Surefire methods for developing quotable quotes
- Techniques for fine tuning nonverbal performance
- How to conduct yourself when interviewed on a podcast
- Role playing practice ideas when you can't meet face-to-face
- Roadblocks to success – like stage fright – and how to overcome them

I realize this chapter will become dated. If you are reading it years after publication, you may find the advice no longer applies. That will be a good thing if we are back to a world sans masks, and with such everyday pleasures as restaurant dining, baseball, theater, and hugs.

CHAPTER 9

The Kicker

Executives who face the press hold their company's future in their hands. A positive attitude and sense of opportunity need to become second nature in order to succeed in business deals with the press. One slip of the tongue or one sideways glance at a reporter can leave a reputation in tatters. This holds both for your personal status and that of your business.

Media relations staffers face similar pressures when counseling spokespeople and dealing with reporters. Building magnetic messages, granting interviews to the press, issuing news releases, and engaging on digital media all take talent and a commitment to improvement over the long run.

Putting the Puzzle Together

Understanding what the media need and when they need it can be puzzling for spokespeople and the communications staff and consultants who advise them. You need and deserve a ready, easy-to-reference resource that spells out how to deal with the media.

This book represents a humble attempt to empower readers with the strategies and tactics you need to build an effective media relations effort for your business.

C-suite executives, issue experts, other corporate and association spokespeople, and media relations professionals can use the commonsense advice found in these pages to move toward achievement of business and public policy goals.

Whether you find yourself in the morass of an all-encompassing crisis like the coronavirus or your reaction to the Black Lives Matter marches, or you are knee deep in day-to-day media interviews, you need to stay up to speed with best communications practices.

Build that solid base with a comprehensive strategic media training regimen. That does not mean just checking a box and calling it a day. A meaningful approach demands a sustained professional development program delivered over time.

It involves sharpening skills in both formal and informal settings. You might begin with a half-day workshop led by an experienced media strategy and training consultant, then follow up with such steps as Q&A sessions with your chief communications officer or periodic telephone refreshers with your consultant. It also might mean helping to guide less experienced colleagues – potential spokespeople – to see how they perform and if they have what it takes to meet the media. Interacting with reporters is not a role everyone can handle, so be selective. And be sure to get your consultant's input; they should be capable of giving you an informed and impartial opinion.

People Power

Gain an understanding of what reporters need from you, both in general and as it pertains to individual newspeople. Never forget that deadlines are sacred and that reporters are under tremendous pressures in terms of resources, time, and the vagaries of editors and news directors.

Related to this, how your company structures its communications shop is important. Plainly put, you should advocate that ex-reporters must be present – experts who have breathed the rarified air of a newsroom and know firsthand how journalism works. It has long baffled me how some companies try to sneak by without this capability. It is akin to hiring someone to translate English to Spanish who has never spoken the language.

Also, your media relations shop needs to be helmed by an adult not afraid to speak truth to power. Advocate for this, too. The individual must have the ability to lay it on the line, telling the C-suite when they are off the mark. It may be a poor messaging idea or a fatal strategic decision. Regardless, your chief communications officer must have the backbone to point out potential pitfalls. Will they have the final say? No. A consummate professional realizes that the CEO is the ultimate decision maker. But they do need to send up a flare when they think a problem exists.

Your chief communicator should also have a solid media strategy and training consultant on speed dial (better yet, on retainer). While your staff has (or should have) intimate knowledge of your day-to-day workings, a skilled consultant can bring added perspectives gained from years of experience across a variety of events and client profiles. Smart companies put this depth of knowledge to work for their benefit.

Remain Vigilant

Note well the techniques reporters might use to trick you. Yes, they may on occasion try to get you to reveal something you'd rather not give up. They may interrupt you, try to put negative words in your mouth, or pause and let an uncomfortable silence linger. Recognize these techniques for what they are. Refuse to fall victim to them.

That said, I do not mean to leave the impression that every encounter with a reporter will prove confrontational. Far from it. In the vast majority of cases – unless you are managing a crisis – the reporter is merely trying to learn your point of view and disseminate it to the public. That's a good thing from your perspective. Your advance preparations should tell you when an interview could turn contentious. Again, these situations are rare, so don't enter into all of your interviews thinking you need a suit of armor. Stay alert? Absolutely. Expect a blow to the midsection every time? No.

Pay attention to the various interview formats you may face, and how to prepare for each. An interview with *The Washington Post* has a different feel than a satellite media tour with television stations nationwide. A podcast appearance is unlike a sit-down with the trade press journalist who covers you routinely. Get a grasp on these distinctions and proceed accordingly.

A reminder about off the record interviews is in order, for some spokespeople try to navigate these ground rules on their own. Bad idea. Leave those negotiations to your media relations staffers. Earlier, we discussed the dissimilarities among off the record, on background, and not for attribution. As you know now, they mean markedly different things. The easiest approach? Stay on the record unless your company has a compelling reason to act otherwise. That has the benefit of making your life less complicated.

In the End, It's a Business Deal

We have spent significant time here discussing how to prepare for an interview. This involves more than just knowing the reporters and their proclivities. It also means mastering the mechanics of this business deal. Approach your sustained professional development program with a scholarly mindset. Participate in Q&A rehearsals with gusto. Pay attention to your nonverbal tools, for reporters as a group tend to note what you are "saying" in that regard. And, of course, internalize your message so you are able to verbalize it.

Let us return one more time to our old friend, messaging. I cannot emphasize enough the important role this plays in your media success. It is challenging to craft the perfectly magnetic message. There is no single right way to do it. This frustrates all of us – spokespeople, media relations staff, and media strategy and training consultants.

I strongly advise you to stay on guard against those who have their black box formulas. In my observations of more than two decades, these are mostly garbage. Think of it this way: If there was only one correct way to develop a message, wouldn't everyone use the exact same methodology?

It takes experience and a depth of knowledge to understand the proper method for structuring the message surrounding a particular issue – your issue. Never let someone try to cram you into a pre-ordained box. You should demand a customized approach.

Sustained professional development is critical in any professional endeavor. No matter how experienced you may be navigating the rush hour traffic you encounter when you deal with reporters, we all have room for improvement.

That is why you are holding this book in your hands. You have learned about essentials like how to prepare for meeting the press, deal with the parry and thrust of Q&A, take charge during the interview, compose your magnetic message, maximize your nonverbal skills, and gain a winning attitude.

Treat this as the one-stop reference you consult prior to engaging in every media interview. Use it often. Consider it your own personal professional development guide. After all, your business and public policy success hang in the balance.

INDEX

ABOUT THE AUTHOR

Communications strategy consultant and author Ed Barks works with communications and government relations executives who counsel their C-suite leaders, and with businesses that need their communications strategy and messaging to deliver bottom line results. They gain an enhanced reputation, greater confidence, more opportunities for career advancement, and achievement of long-term business and public policy goals.

Ed is the author of two previous books: *A+ Strategies for C-Suite Communications: Turning Today's Leaders into Tomorrow's Influencers* and *The Truth About Public Speaking: The Three Keys to Great Presentations.*

He contributes to a variety of publications and is the former "Speaking Sense" columnist for the *Washington Business Journal.* He has published numerous additional works such as:

- "Eleven Elements to Mold a Magnetic Message: How to Shape Your Story for the Press, Policymakers, and the Public"
- "Beyond the Bottom Line: 20 Ways to Reduce Reputational Risk"
- "Thrill on the Hill: How to Turn Congressional Testimony into Public Policy Success"
- "The Lasting Effects of Media Training: Lifelong Learning or Temporary Phenomenon?"

More than 5,000 business leaders, association executives, scientists, government officials, entertainers, and other thought leaders can thank Ed for sharpening their communications edge.

According to his clients, he "knows how to elicit peak performance."

They call him "a master at connecting with his audience" and "an effective educator," and give his communications training workshops "two thumbs up!"

Ed founded Barks Communications in 1997. He has held leadership roles including service on the Board of Governors of the National Press Club, the faculty of the U.S. Chamber of Commerce Institute for Organization Management, the Board of Directors of the Institute of Management Consultants National Capital Region, and the Consultants Section Council of the American Society of Association Executives' (ASAE).

An inside-the-Beltway veteran, Ed has spent more than three decades in Washington, D.C. He brings another critical perspective to his clients' communications needs – that of a former broadcaster and journalist. He knows firsthand the tricks and techniques of the reporting trade, thanks to a decade of experience in radio broadcasting.

Ed also created the C-suite Blueprint blog community for communications and government relations executives who advise their C-suite leaders.

He lives in the Washington, D.C., area with his wife, Celeste. His daughter, Polly, is a sustainability and zero waste consultant in Indiana.

CONTACT ED BARKS

Ed loves to hear from his readers. Here's how you can get in touch:

- Visit him at www.barkscomm.com
- Get strategy updates at the C-suite Blueprint blog: csuiteblue-print.wordpress.com.
- Join his Communications Community at www.barkscomm.com/comms-community
- Follow Ed on Twitter at www.twitter.com/EdBarks
- Subscribe to his YouTube channel, Communications Strategy TV, at http://bit.ly/CommsStrategyTV
- Follow his Goodreads author page at www.goodreads.com/EdBarks (while you're there, send him a "Friend" invitation; he will gladly accept)

To contact Ed directly (he answers his own phone and email):

- Email: ebarks@barkscomm.com
- Phone: (540) 955-0600

Now that you've read *Reporters Don't Hate You*, Ed would be most appreciative if you posted your honest review at your favorite online bookseller.

Spreading the word on your digital media channels is also welcomed.

Buy Ed's other books, *A+ Strategies for C-Suite Communications: Turning Today's Leaders into Tomorrow's Influencers* and *The Truth About*

Public Speaking: The Three Keys to Great Presentations, both available in paperback and ebook formats at www.barkscomm.com/eds-books.

Do you want to keep pace with the latest from Ed, including inside information on his forthcoming books? Sign up for his Communications Community newsletter at www.barkscomm.com/comms-community.

Ed enjoys sharing ideas with audiences large and small, for example, your:

- C-suite leadership
- Board of directors
- Communications team
- Government relations team
- Entire staff during employee development day
- Association annual meeting
- Professional society's monthly program
- Business book club

To arrange either a live or remote speaking engagement with Ed, visit www.barkscomm.com/speaker or call (540) 955-0600.

Made in the USA
Middletown, DE
08 August 2020